101
Ways to
Finish
Wood

Edited by Jeanne Stauffer

HOUSE of
WHITE
BIRCHES
PUBLISHERS
SINCE 1947

Woodworking for Women®
101 Ways to Finish Wood

Copyright © 2005 House of White Birches, Berne, Indiana 46711
Woodworking for Women™ is a trademark of DRG Texas LP,
licensed for use by House of White Birches.

Editor: Jeanne Stauffer
Art Director: Brad Snow
Publishing Services Manager: Brenda Gallmeyer
Associate Editors: Sue Reeves, Dianne Schmidt
Technical Editors: Marla Freeman, Amy Phillips
Copy Supervisor: Michelle Beck
Copy Editor: Conor Allen

Photography: Tammy Christian, Carl Clark, Christena Green, Justin Wiard
Photography Stylist: Tammy Nussbaum

Graphic Arts Supervisor: Ronda Bechinski
Book Design/Graphic Artist: Amy S. Lin
Production Assistant: Marj Morgan
Traffic Coordinator: Sandra Beres
Technical Artist: John Buskirk, Chad Summers

Chief Executive Officer: John Robinson
Publishing Director: David McKee
Book Marketing Director: Craig Scott
Sales Director: John Boggs
Editorial Director: Vivian Rothe
Publishing Services Director: Brenda R. Wendling

Printed in China
First Printing: 2005
Library of Congress Number: 2004106062
Hardcover ISBN: 1-931171-98-X
Softcover ISBN: 1-59635-011-3

Every effort has been made to ensure the accuracy and completeness of the
instructions in this book. However, we cannot be responsible for human error
or for the results when using materials other than those specified in the
instructions, or for variations in individual work.

Important Safety Notice: To prevent accidents, read instructions and use all safety
guards on power equipment. Wear safety goggles and headphones to protect yourself.
Do not wear loose clothing when working on power equipment. Due to the variability
of construction materials and skill levels, neither the staff nor the publisher of
Woodworking for Women books assumes any responsibility for any accidents, injuries,
damages or other losses incurred resulting from the material presented in this book.

Welcome

The construction of any woodworking project, large or small, is very rewarding and always gives a sense of accomplishment. Once the project is made and is sitting there in the shop, ready to finish, the fun begins.

There are so many ways you can finish a woodworking project. Certainly, the first choice is whether or not you want a finish that shows off the beauty of the wood. If you decide on a wood finish, there are many choices. Do you want to stain the wood or use a clear finish? Whatever your choice, we have included several products that you can use, each one using a different method of application.

Wood is beautiful, but some projects need a special finish to look truly inspired. If you decide to try something other than a wood finish, the sky is the limit. There are so many paints, faux finishes, techniques and methods that we barely scratch the surface in this book.

To see the difference a finish can make, look at the projects in this book. We have taken the same project and finished it in several different ways. Some individual projects use several finishing techniques. No matter, each finish gives the project a totally different look.

So now it's time to start. Pick a project to make, select a finish for that project and you are ready for hours of fun. Before you know it, you'll be finished with the first project and ready to start the second.

Happy woodworking,

CONTENTS

PRETTY
PLANT STANDS

Designs by Anna Thompson

Easy dowelled joints make this stand sturdy yet simple to make. The classic lines and single drawer make this a welcome addition to any room.

CUTTING

1 From 2x2 oak, cut four 32-inch lengths (B) for legs.

2 From 1x6-inch oak board, cut three 5½-inch lengths (A) for back and sides.

3 From 1x2 oak, cut four 5½-inch lengths (C) for braces.

4 From 1x1 oak, cut four 5½-inch lengths (D) for drawer runners and top cleats.

5 Rip a piece of ½-inch Baltic birch plywood to 4x30 inches. Raise the table saw blade ¼ inch and set the fence ½ inch from the blade; cut a ¼x¼-inch groove ½ inch from one long edge of 4-inch-wide strip. From grooved strip, cut two 6¼-inch lengths (G) for drawer sides, and two 4½-inch lengths (H) for drawer back and front.

6 From ¼-inch plywood, cut a 5x5¾-inch piece (F) for drawer bottom.

7 Using router and 45-degree bevel bit, bevel top edge of ¾x5½x6-inch oak board for front (I) and ¾x10¾x10¾-inch oak piece for top (E).

ASSEMBLE

1 Referring to Fig. 1 and assembly diagram (pages 8 & 9), lay out pieces and mark dowel locations on outside faces of boards using carpenter's square and a sharp pencil; clearly label each joint.

2 Drill back and sides (A), legs (B) and braces (C) for dowels. Insert dowel pins and dry-fit stand; glue joints, clamp and let dry.

3 Attach each of two drawer runners (D) to bottom edge of side using two screws. *Note: Drill pilot holes and countersink all screws.* Glue top cleats (D) to top edges of sides; clamp and let dry.

4 Position top (E) on stand and attach with remaining screws through top cleats.

5 Insert 5-inch ends of drawer bottom (F) into grooves on drawer back and front (H). Then insert 5¾-inch sides of drawer bottom (F) into grooves on drawer sides (G). Glue and nail drawer sides to front and back.

PROJECT SIZE
10¾x33x10¾ inches

TOOLS
- Table saw or crosscut handsaw
- Router with 45-degree bevel router bit
- Carpenter's square
- Drill
- Self-centering dowel jig
- Clamps

SUPPLIES FOR ONE STAND
- 2x2 oak: 12 feet
- 1x6 oak: 2 feet
- 1x2 oak: 3 feet
- 1x1 oak: 3 feet
- ½x6x30-inch Baltic birch plywood
- ¼x6x12-inch scrap plywood
- ¾x5½x6-inch oak board*
- ¾x10¾x10¾-inch oak*

- Twenty ⅜-inch dowel pins
- Wood glue
- Six 1¼-inch wood screws
- Finish nails
- Double-sided carpet tape
- 1¼-inch wooden knob with screw

Measurement given is actual, not nominal. Standard nominal lumber will need to be ripped to size.

For Natural Oak Plant Stand
- Deft clear Danish oil finish

For Sunroom Plant Stand
- White semigloss latex wall paint and soft cloth

For Art Deco Plant Stand
- Wood Kote black Jel'd Stain and soft, lint-free cloth
- Deft semigloss lacquer

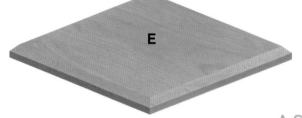

ASSEMBLY DIAGRAM

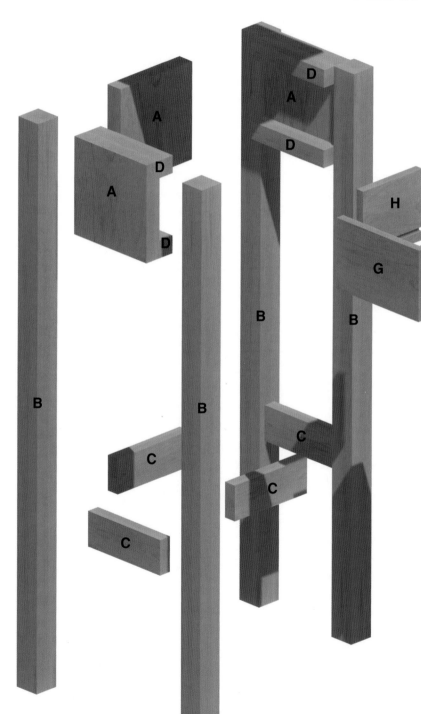

PRETTY PLANT STANDS CUTTING CHART
(Actual Sizes)

P	T	W	L	#
A	¾"	5½"	5½"	3
B	1½"	1½"	32"	4
C	¾"	1½"	5½"	4
D	¾"	¾"	5½"	4
E	¾"	10¾"	10¾"	1
F	¼"	5"	5¾"	1
G	½"	4"	6¼"	2
H	½"	4"	4½"	2
I	¾"	5½"	6"	1

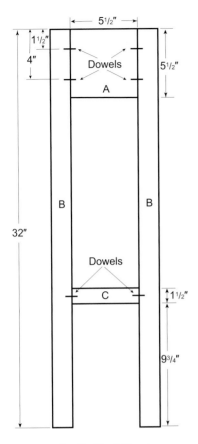

**Pretty Plant Stands
Side/Back View
Fig. 1**

6 Slide drawer into place. Attach front (I) to drawer front (H) using double-sided carpet tape. Remove drawer. Mark placement of knob and drill hole for screw; attach knob.

Finishes

NATURAL OAK PLANT STAND

1 Following manufacturer's directions, apply clear oil finish to wood; allow to penetrate for 30 minutes, then wipe off excess and let dry. Repeat at least three times. ***Note:*** *If excess oil is not completely wiped off and becomes tacky, simply apply more oil and repeat the process.*

SUNROOM PLANT STAND

1 Thin latex wall paint with water, then apply to stand with a cloth. Repeat as needed to achieve desired finish.

ART DECO PLANT STAND

1 Use a soft, lint-free cloth to wipe on three coats of black Jel'd Stain, letting dry thoroughly after each coat.

2 Following manufacturer's directions, spray stand with three coats of semigloss lacquer. ❋

NATURAL OAK PLANT STAND

1 DANISH OIL

The clear oil finish by Deft penetrates the wood, making it resistant to drips and condensation. Because the finish is in the wood, not on top of it, there is nothing to chip, crack or peel, preserving the natural beauty of the wood texture.

SUNROOM PLANT STAND

2 DO-IT-YOURSELF WHITEWASH

Mix regular semigloss latex wall paint with water to achieve a thin consistency, then wipe it onto the surface of the wood with a soft cloth until desired effect is achieved.

3 WIPE-ON BLACK STAIN

Wipe on three coats of Wood-Kote black stain with a soft, lint-free cloth to obtain the deep, rich color. Staining is a common way to add color to light wood.

ART DECO PLANT STAND

4 SEMIGLOSS LACQUER

This Deft product can be applied with a brush or sprayed on for a baby-safe, fast-drying, crystal-clear finish on furniture, cabinets, paneling, antiques and crafts.

SPINDLE SHELF NOOK

Designs by Barbara Greve

Change the personality of this piece by changing the shelves to match your mood and decor. From wild to whimsical, these finishes will fit your style.

PROJECT SIZE
12x20½x7 inches

TOOLS
- Scroll saw or jigsaw
- Drill with wood bits, including ⅝-inch bit
- Bar clamp
- 1/32-inch nail set

SUPPLIES FOR ONE NOOK AND ONE SET OF SHELVES
- ½x5½-inch pine*: 6 feet
- ½x7x12-inch scrap plywood
- 1⅜x3-inch pine*: 18 inches
- ½x4-inch pine*: 2 feet
- ⅛x12x20-inch scrap plywood
- Two 17x1¼-inch wooden spindles
- Plain white paper
- Graphite paper
- Sandpaper
- Wood glue
- #18x¾-inch wire nails
- #4x⅝-inch wood screws
- Wood putty

*Measurements given are actual, not nominal. Standard nominal lumber will need to be ripped to size.

For Snakeskin Shelf
- Acrylic paint: Americana acrylic paint from DecoArt: titanium white #DA01, sand #DA04, light buttermilk #DA164, terra-cotta #DA62, French vanilla #DA184, true ochre #DA143 and burnt sienna #DA63
- Satin varnish
- Americana primary yellow #DA201 spray paint from DecoArt
- Two 13x6-inch pieces of aluminum diamond-mesh gutter guard
- Small sea sponge
- Craft knife

For Denim Look Shelf
- Acrylic paint: Americana acrylic paint from DecoArt: titanium white #DA01, sand #D04A, light buttermilk #DA164, winter blue #DA190 and uniform blue #DA86
- Satin varnish
- Two 13x6-inch pieces burlap
- Drywall sealer
- Clear Gel Stain #DS31 from DecoArt
- Paper towels
- Stiff-bristled brush
- Matte varnish

For Roller Spots Shelf
- Acrylic paint: Americana acrylic paint from DecoArt: titanium white #DA01, sand #D04A, light buttermilk #DA164, golden straw #DA168, silver sage green #DA149, gingerbread #DA218 and rookwood red #DA97
- Satin varnish
- 3-inch trim roller
- Liner paintbrush
- Matte varnish

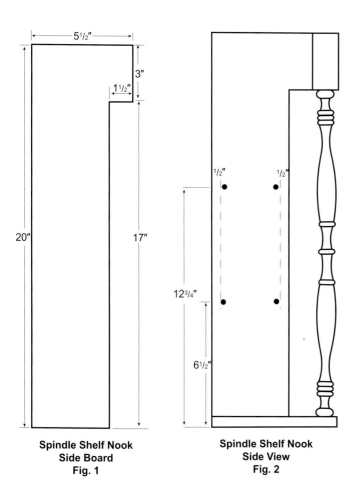

**Spindle Shelf Nook
Side Board
Fig. 1**

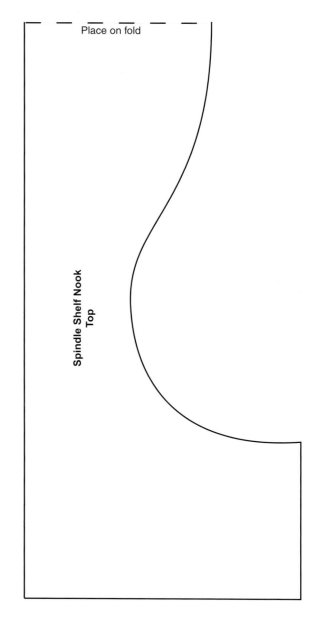

**Spindle Shelf Nook
Side View
Fig. 2**

Place on fold

**Spindle Shelf Nook
Top**

CUTTING

1 From ½x5½-inch pine board, cut one 11-inch length (A) for top and two 20-inch lengths (C) for sides. Beginning 3 inches from top edge of each side, draw a vertical line 1½ inches from one side; beginning at this line, draw a horizontal line to edge of board 3 inches from top (Fig. 1). Cut out L shape.

2 From ½-inch scrap plywood, cut a 7x12-inch piece (B) for bottom. Using ⅝-inch bit, drill a hole into each front corner centered at a point ⅝ inch from each side and ⅝ inch from front edge, for inserting spindles.

3 From 1⅜x3-inch pine, cut a 12-inch length (D) for front. Trace pattern for top onto folded paper to make a full-size pattern. Use graphite paper to transfer lines to piece D and cut out. Using ⅝-inch bit, drill holes for inserting spindles in bottom edge, centered on each side and ¾ inch from front edge.

4 Using ½x4-inch pine, cut two 10⅞-inch lengths (E) for shelves.

5 From ⅛-inch scrap plywood, cut a 12x20-inch piece (F) for back.

ASSEMBLE & FINISH NOOK

1 Referring to assembly diagram, glue and nail top (A) and bottom (B) to sides (C). Apply glue to spindle tenons and insert into drilled holes on bottom (B) and front (D). Clamp in place and let dry.

2 Glue and nail back in place; let dry. Referring to Fig. 2, drill pilot holes for screws in each side (C). With shelf held firmly in place, drive in screws. Repeat for second shelf.

Project note: *If desired, do not permanently attach these shelves, so you can change easily.*

ASSEMBLY DIAGRAM

SPINDLE SHELF NOOK CUTTING CHART
(Actual Sizes)

P	T	W	L	#
A	½"	5½"	11"	1
B	½"	7"	12"	1
C	½"	5½"	20"	2
D	1⅜"	3"	12"	1
E	½"	4"	10⅞"	2
F	⅛"	12"	20"	1

3 Set nails and fill nail holes with wood putty; let dry and sand smooth. Remove dust.

4 Mix equal parts titanium white, light buttermilk and sand; apply at least two coats to nook, letting dry after each coat.

5 Apply two coats of satin varnish, letting dry after each coat.

Finishes

SNAKESKIN SHELF

1 Base-coat shelves with titanium white.

2 Wrap aluminum diamond-mesh gutter guard tightly around each shelf and spray with primary yellow; let dry.

3 Using sea sponge, lightly dab over mesh with terra-cotta to create alternating large diamond shapes across the shelf.

4 Lightly dab between terra-cotta diamond shapes with a mixture of equal amounts French vanilla and titanium white, then randomly dab over mesh with true ochre.

5 Dab burnt sienna lightly in middle of each terra-cotta diamond to darken. Let dry.

6 Remove wire mesh. Remove excess paint with craft knife to define diamond shapes more clearly.

5 SNAKESKIN

DecoArt Americana acrylic spray paint applied through a large screen gives the scaly appearance of reptile skin.

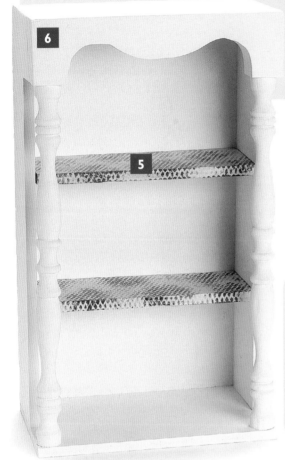

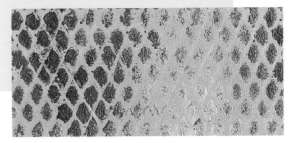

SNAKESKIN SHELF

6 ACRYLIC PAINT

Water-based and nontoxic, DecoArt's Americana acrylic paint is an all-purpose paint for decorative painting, home décor and general craft painting for use on almost any surface.

ROLLER SPOTS SHELF

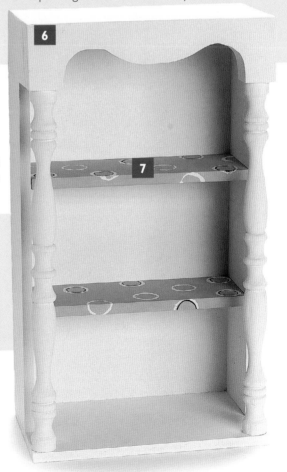

7 ROLLER SPOTS

The open end of an average paint roller produces a funky, freeform pattern in acrylic paint.

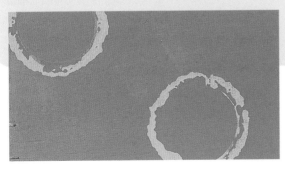

7 Apply two coats of satin varnish, letting dry after each coat.

DENIM LOOK SHELF

1 Paint burlap with drywall sealer mixed with two parts water; let dry.

2 Base-coat shelves with a mixture of equal parts titanium white, light buttermilk and sand; let dry.

3 Apply a coat of winter blue to shelf; lay burlap on top and apply pressure to imprint burlap texture. Remove burlap and let dry.

4 Mix one part uniform blue with one part clear gel stain and apply to shelf. Wipe off with paper towels until a thin layer remains. Drag a stiff-bristled brush over stain to make subtle striations horizontally, then vertically. Let dry.

5 Randomly dry-brush titanium white across shelf. Using fine-grit sandpaper, lightly sand random areas to give a worn denim effect.

6 Apply two coats of matte varnish, letting dry after each coat.

ROLLER SPOTS SHELF

1 Base-coat shelves with golden straw; let dry.

2 Mix equal parts sand, titanium white and light buttermilk; load circular end of trim roller with mixture and stamp randomly across shelf, reloading as necessary. Let dry.

6 ACRYLIC PAINT

Water-based and nontoxic, DecoArt's Americana acrylic paint is an all-purpose paint for decorative painting, home décor and general craft painting for use on almost any surface.

**DENIM LOOK
SHELF**

8 DENIM

Burlap strips are stiffened with drywall sealer, then pressed onto wet acrylic paint to imprint the texture.

3 Using liner paintbrush, outline inside of each stamped circle using silver sage green, gingerbread and rookwood red in random patterns. If desired, leave a couple circles without outlines. Let dry.

4 Apply two coats of matte varnish, letting dry after each coat. ❋

9 GEL STAINS

Add subtle striations using a stiff-bristled brush and acrylic paint mixed with DecoArt Gel Stain. This translucent gel stain has a thick, creamy texture.

ALL-OCCASION SIGNS

Designs by Loretta Mateik

Welcome visitors to your home, accent your garden or provide a place for youngsters to hang their hats—these small, decorative signs are just the thing you need to personalize your space.

CUTTING

1 Use table saw to cut ½-inch plywood into one 2-inch-wide x 12-inch strip and two ⅝-inch-wide x 12-inch strips. Cut ⅝-inch-wide strips into one 11¼-inch-long strip for border bottom and two 3-inch-long strips for border sides.

2 Cut 2-inch-wide strip into an 11¼-inch length for border top. Use graphite paper to transfer top border pattern (page 27) to border top. Using scroll saw, cut bottom edge of border top (along solid curved line) only.

3 From ⅛-inch plywood, cut a piece 11¼x5⅝ inches for sign back.

ASSEMBLE

1 Working from the back of the sign, glue and nail bottom and side border pieces to front of sign back, then glue and nail top border piece in place (Fig. 1, page 25).

2 Following dashed pattern line, use scroll saw to cut out top edge of top border through all thicknesses.

3 Set nails and fill holes with wood putty; let dry. Sand all surfaces smooth and wipe clean.

PROJECT SIZE
11⅛x5⅝x⅝ inches

TOOLS
- Table saw
- Scroll saw or jigsaw
- Drill with 7⁄64-inch bit
- Nail set
- Stylus

SUPPLIES FOR ONE SIGN
- ½x6x12-inch Baltic birch plywood
- ⅛x6x12-inch Baltic birch plywood
- Wood glue
- ½-inch brads
- Wood putty
- Sandpaper

For Garden Sign
- Masking tape and paper
- Ceramcoat acrylic paint from Delta: blue heaven #2037, Indiana rose #2018, moss green #2570, red iron oxide #2020, Cape Cod blue #2133, dark forest green #2096, yellow #2504, raspberry #2520, brown iron oxide #2023, black #2506, green sea #2445, tangerine #2043, antique gold #2002 and light ivory #2401
- Paintbrushes
- Make It Stone rose quartz #18204 textured paint spray from Krylon
- Graphite paper
- Stipple paintbrush
- Eraser
- Matte spray varnish

For Kid's Door Sign
- Two 1⅜-inch wooden axle pegs
- Ceramcoat acrylic paint from Delta: lilac #2060 and vintage wine #2434
- Paintbrushes
- Child's signature
- Graphite paper
- Purple Permapaque Paint Marker from Sakura
- Eraser
- Satin Clear Wood Finish varnish from Krylon

For Welcome Sign
- Masking tape and paper
- Brilliant Gold metallic spray paint by Design Master
- Ceramcoat acrylic paint from Delta: antique white #2001
- ¾-inch flat wash paintbrush
- Sharpie Metallic gold fine-point pen
- Black Scratch Pad Alphabet #41-7502 rub-on letters from Provo Craft
- Eraser
- Matte spray varnish
- Sandpaper

10 STONE TEXTURED LOOK

This spray finish produces a beautiful stone-textured look on almost any surface. It's quick and easy to apply to pottery and planters as well as picture frames and furniture.

11 STIPPLING

Delta Ceramcoat acrylic paint and special stippling brushes give an Impressionistic feel to this decorative sign. The bristles of a stippling brush are quite stiff, allowing the brush to bounce on the set surface of the paint to create the effect.

GARDEN SIGN

Finishes

GARDEN SIGN

1 Completely mask off inside of sign using masking tape and paper. Brush on one coat of Indiana rose to back and sign borders; let dry.

2 Following manufacturer's directions, apply rose quartz Make-It-Stone to sign borders, repeating application until desired effect is achieved. Let dry.

3 Remove mask from inside sign. Lightly transfer a horizontal line across sign to distinguish sky and garden areas. Base-coat sky with blue heaven and garden with dark forest green; apply multiple coats as needed to cover. Let dry.

4 Transfer garden pattern to sign using graphite paper and stylus. *Note: Transfer lines for clouds and foliage very lightly, or use only as reference and paint freehand.* Paint as follows:

Heart-shaped birdhouse—Base-coat with *Indiana rose*. Paint roof with *red iron oxide*; paint pole with *brown*

iron oxide. Add detail lines with *light ivory*. Paint flower on birdhouse with *Cape Cod blue* with *green sea* leaves and a *yellow* center. Lightly shade around outside edge of birdhouse with *red iron oxide*. Dot the opening with *black*.

Square birdhouse—Base-coat with *tangerine*. With *red iron oxide*, paint roof, platform line under birdhouse, perch extending from side of birdhouse and lines on house. Paint pole with *brown iron oxide*. Shade left side of house with *red iron oxide*. Dot

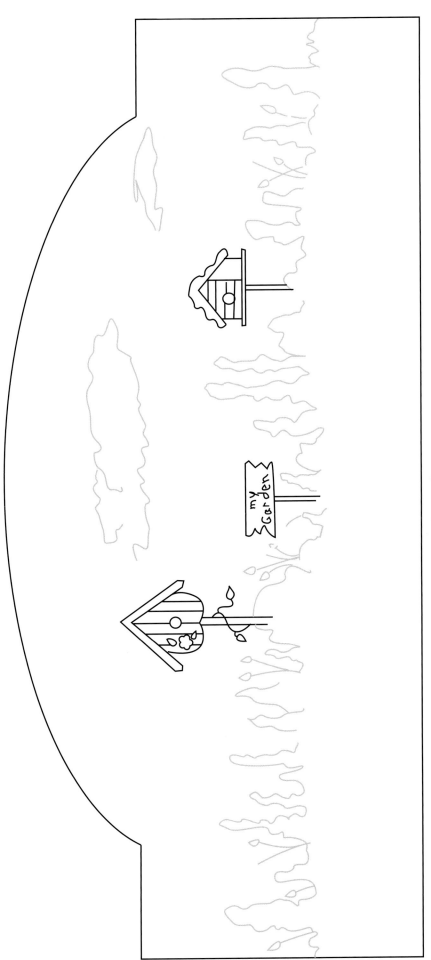

Garden Sign
Garden Pattern

12 CLEAR UV PROTECTANT

This finish is durable, non-toxic and weatherproof, so it can be used indoors or out.

13 PAINT MARKERS

Permapaque Fine-Point markers are great for detailed designs and lettering anywhere a permanent opaque marker is needed. They are odorless and safe for kids to use.

KID'S DOOR SIGN

opening with *black*.

Small sign—Base-coat with *light ivory*. Paint pole with *brown iron oxide*. Letter "My Garden" with *black*.

Garden area—Using *dark forest green* and stipple brush, stipple in uneven green areas. Randomly stipple garden area again using *green sea*, creating small bushlike areas. Continue stippling in same manner using *yellow*, *tangerine*, *Indiana rose*, *blue*

heaven and *light ivory*. **Note:** *At the beginning this may look messy or disjointed, but continue stippling and soon it will resemble a garden.*

Stems and vines—Using *dark forest green* and *moss green*, add grasslike stems here and there, and the vine climbing up the birdhouse pole. With *raspberry*, st ipple in two tall stalklike stems, then dot with *Indiana rose* and liner brush. Use *dark forest green* to add leaves to

the vine on the birdhouse.

Stem flowers—Use *light ivory*, *raspberry* and *antique gold* with a round brush to add tiny flowers to ends of grasslike stems by lightly touching ends of stems.

Clouds—Using *light ivory* and an angled paintbrush, apply clouds with a shaky, exaggerated motion. Soften the edges with a mop brush.

5 Erase any pattern lines that may still be visible. Spray with several light coats of matte varnish, letting dry after each coat.

KID'S DOOR SIGN

1 For placement of wooden pegs, drill two $\frac{7}{64}$-inch holes $\frac{3}{8}$-inch deep on border bottom, $2\frac{1}{2}$ inches from each edge. Sand all surfaces smooth and wipe clean.

2 Base-coat inside area of sign with lilac; let dry. Sand and wipe clean. Base-coat again with lilac.

3 Base-coat wooden pegs with vintage wine, applying multiple coats to cover.

4 Use graphite paper and stylus to transfer child's signature to sign. **Note:** *If child cannot write, print name on computer using desired font.*

5 Trace transferred lines with paint marker; let dry.

6 Erase any transfer lines that may still be visible. Glue pegs into holes, sanding lightly to fit, if necessary.

7 Following manufacturer's directions, apply several light coats of Clear Wood varnish, letting dry after each coat.

WELCOME SIGN

1 Completely mask off inside of sign using masking tape and paper. Spray borders of frame with brilliant gold,

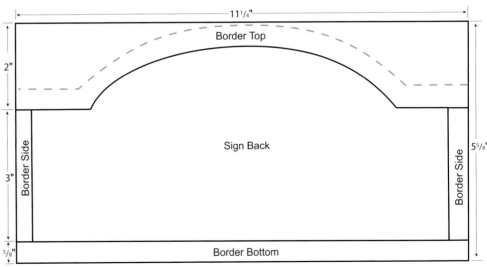

All-Occasion Signs
Fig. 1
Assemble border bottom, sides
and top on sign back, with edges flush.

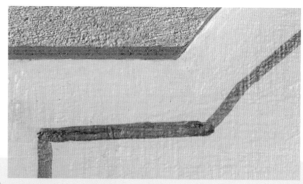

14 GOLD EDGES

Rich, lustrous, spray-on metallic finish by Design Master provides quick coverage in an extra-thin coat.

15 METALLIC GOLD PENS

Create narrow borders easily with a Sharpie permanent metallic gold pen. Thin, thick, straight or curvy, there's no limit to the kinds of lines you can create with a permanent ink pen.

WELCOME SIGN

16 RUB-ON TRANSFER LETTERS

Rub-on transfer letters from Provo Craft let you personalize this sign with any name, house number or greeting.

following manufacturer's directions; let dry. Turn over and spray the back of the sign; let dry. Lightly sand and wipe clean. Apply a second coat; let dry.

2 Remove masking tape. Base-coat inside center area of sign with antique white; let dry. Sand and wipe clean, then repeat.

3 Lightly draw a line around sign approximately ⅜ inch inside borders. Outline with metallic gold pen.

4 Very lightly draw a guideline for applying rub-on letters. Transfer letters to sign following manufacturer's directions.

5 Erase any lines that may still be visible. Following manufacturer's directions, apply several light coats of varnish, letting dry after each coat. ✵

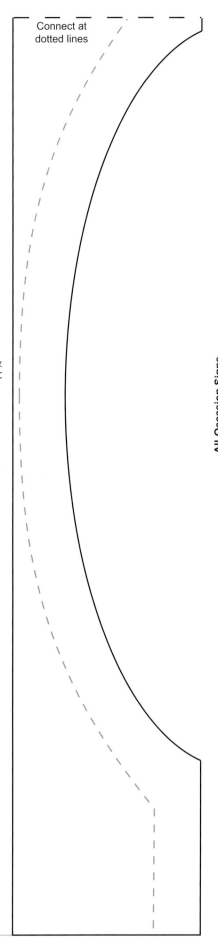

Connect at
dotted lines

11 1/4"

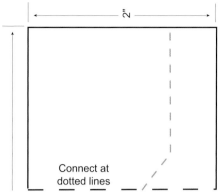

2"

Connect at
dotted lines

**All-Occasion Signs
Sign Top Border**

TRIO OF
BENCHES

Designs by Joyce Atwood

These small benches are perfect for those small, hard-to-decorate areas indoors or on a sheltered patio. Sit on them or display treasured items; they're sure to be a hit anywhere you put them.

CUTTING

1 From 1x10, cut one 24-inch length (for top) and two 17-inch lengths (for legs).

2 Cut 1x4 to 20½-inch length (for brace).

3 Lightly mark a vertical line down center of each leg. Use graphite paper to transfer leg cutout pattern (page 30) onto each leg, aligning center marks; cut out with scroll saw.

4 Using ¼-inch round over bit, rout edges of legs, brace and top.

Note: Do not rout top edges of legs or ends of brace.

ASSEMBLE

Note: Drill pilot holes. Countersink screws for ½-inch furniture buttons.

1 Referring to Fig. 1 (page 30), screw brace to legs.

2 Center top on legs and secure with two screws into each leg.

3 Hammer furniture buttons into screw holes. Remove dust with tack cloth.

Finishes

AMERICANA BENCH

Note: Allow paint to dry after each application.

1 Use foam brush to apply Primer and Stain Blocker to entire bench; let dry.

2 Apply ¾-inch-wide tape around top along outer edge to mask off area for dark ecru stripe; mask off another stripe adjacent to the first (for red stripe). Burnish edges of tape.

PROJECT SIZE
24x17¾x9¼ inches

TOOLS
- Table saw, radial arm saw or crosscut handsaw
- Scroll saw
- Drill
- Router with ¼-inch round over bit
- Palm sander

SUPPLIES FOR ONE BENCH
- 1x10 pine: 6 feet
- 1x4 pine: 3 feet
- Graphite paper
- 1⅝-inch wood screws

- Eight ½-inch wood furniture buttons
- Medium- and fine-grit sandpaper
- Americana Primer and Stain Blocker #DSA34 from DecoArt
- Foam brush

For Americana Bench
- ¾-inch-wide Scotch Magic Tape
- Americana Satin Enamels from DecoArt: evening blue #DSA16, rustic red #DSA42, dark ecru #DSA06 and French blue #DSA43
- Sea sponge
- Star-shaped sponge stamp
- Americana Satins satin varnish #DSA28 from DecoArt

For Embossed Stucco Bench
- Americana Stuccos Texture Tools #DAS132 from DecoArt
- Americana Stuccos textured paint by DecoArt: 3 jars light ecru #AST04
- Stencil spray
- Floral border stencil

For Whitewashed Bench
- Clean, soft cloths
- Americana Water-Based Stain white wash #AMS10 from DecoArt
- Americana Triple Thick Gloss Glaze #TG01 from DecoArt

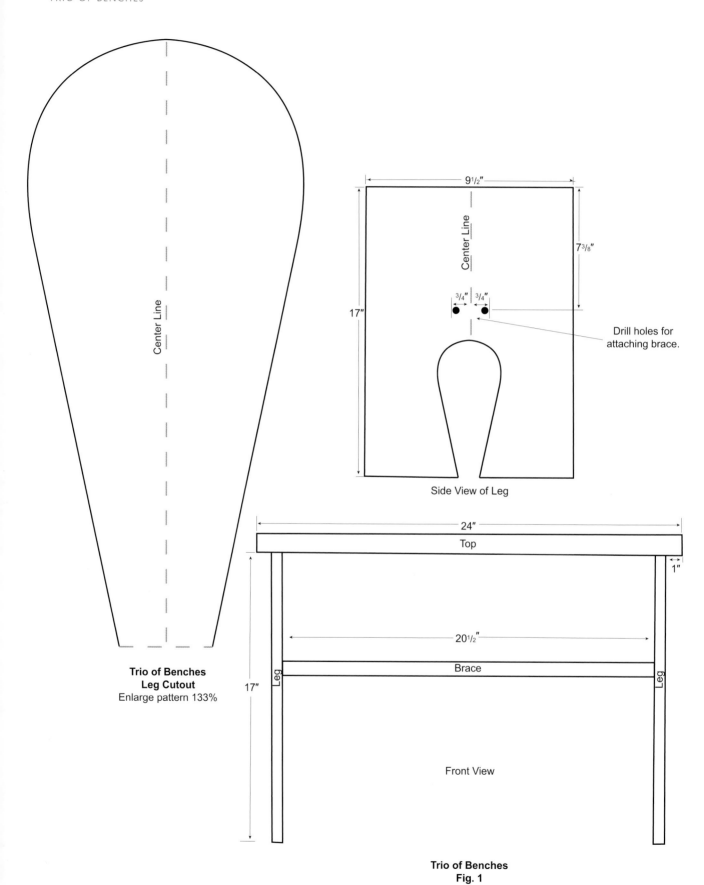

Center Line

9¹/₂"

Center Line

7³/₈"

17"

³/₄" ³/₄"

Drill holes for
attaching brace.

Side View of Leg

**Trio of Benches
Leg Cutout**
Enlarge pattern 133%

24"

Top

1"

20¹/₂"

Leg

Brace

Leg

17"

Front View

**Trio of Benches
Fig. 1**

18 AMERICANA SATINS VARNISH
This varnish by DecoArt goes on smooth and dries to a very hard, durable finish that can stand up to daily use.

17 SHAPED STAMPING
Use a child's star-shaped sponge to stamp the star shapes onto the top of the inch.

AMERICANA
BENCH

19 SEA SPONGE STAMPING
Use a natural sea sponge with Americana acrylic paint by DecoArt to create the textured stripes on this patriotic bench. Americana is water-based and non-toxic, making it suitable for use by children.

3 Paint all exposed areas of bench *except* brace with one coat of evening blue.

4 Dip sea sponge first in evening blue, then in French blue and dab onto bench.

5 Use tape to mask off inside portion of legs adjacent to brace; paint brace with three coats of rustic red. Remove tape.

6 Remove outside strip of tape on top. Mask off edge of bench top, then use 1-inch wash brush to paint stripe with two coats of dark ecru. Remove tape on outer edge of top, and inside strip of tape.

7 Mask off both edges of area for red stripe and apply three coats of rustic red. Remove tape.

8 Dip star-shaped sponge stamp in dark ecru and press onto top to make three stars. Let dry.

9 Apply two coats of satin varnish to entire bench, following manufacturer's directions.

EMBOSSED STUCCO BENCH

1 Use foam brush to apply Primer and Stain Blocker to entire bench; let dry.

2 Working in small areas at a time, use the straight edge of the zigzag texture tool to apply a ⅛-inch thickness of stucco to legs, brace, underside of top and top edge, then use zigzag edge to add texture and design. ***Note:*** *Do not apply stucco to bottoms of legs so bench sits flat.*

3 Using smooth side of texture tool, apply stucco to bench top like creamy cake icing. Let dry.

4 Spray stencil and position on top of bench. Smooth stucco over stencil, then carefully remove stencil; let dry. Reposition stencil and repeat process to achieve desired design. Let dry 72 hours.

5 Lightly sand top of bench to remove some of the rough spots; sand around buttons. Remove dust.

WHITEWASHED BENCH

1 Lightly dampen bench with water; let dry. Sand surface with medium-grit sandpaper, then a fine-grit sandpaper and remove dust.

2 Apply Stain Conditioner with foam brush; remove excess with a clean cloth. Let dry 30 minutes.

3 With a soft cloth, apply white wash stain to bench; let dry. Apply a second coat; let dry.

4 Spray with two coats of Triple Glaze Spray following manufacturer's directions. ❁

20 STUCCO STENCIL

A stencil and Americana Stucco from DecoArt are all you need to create an elegant embossed pattern on the top of this decorative bench. Simply smooth a layer of stucco over the stencil and lift—the stucco will retain the stencil's shape as it dries.

21 ZIGZAG STUCCO

Create the ridges on the legs of this bench using a zigzag stucco tool and Americana Stucco, a heavy-bodied textural paint from DecoArt.

20

21

EMBOSSED STUCCO BENCH

23 STAIN BLOCKER

Stain blocker seals the wood surface and prevents water or tannin stains from bleeding through the finish.

22 PRIMER

Primer is the initial coat of paint or sealant applied to a surface in preparation for painting. The primer seals the surface of wood and provides a good base for additional finishes.

25 TRIPLE THICK GLAZE

This spray finish by DecoArt creates a thick, clear acrylic coating to give a glass-like illusion of depth. It goes on smoothly, dries quickly, will not yellow and is nontoxic.

24 WHITEWASH

Nontoxic and quick-drying, Americana water-based stains by DecoArt produce a translucent finish and cleans up easily with soap and water.

24

25

26

WHITEWASHED BENCH

26 STAIN CONDITIONER

To reduce splotching and uneven staining when finishing soft woods such as pine, use a wood conditioner to partially seal the surface.

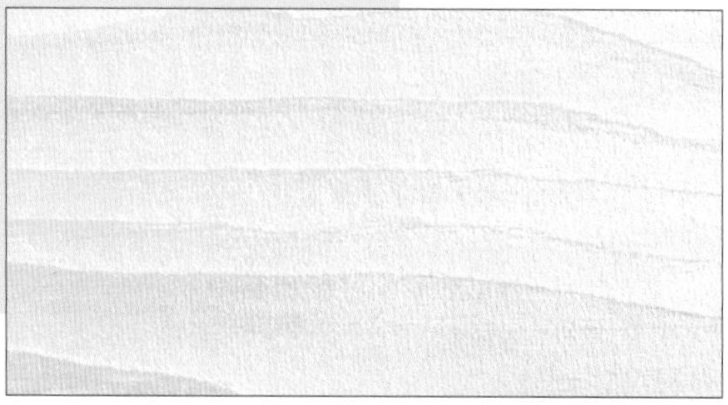

FAMILY OF FRAMES

Designs by LuAnn Nelson

Display your treasured photos in frames as special as they are! We show you eight variations, but the possibilities for this little project are endless.

CUTTING

1 Set table saw blade at a height of ¼ inch. Run 1x4 through table saw to make a rabbet on one edge.

2 Cut 1x4 into four 12-inch lengths. Mark a 45-degree angle at each end of each length (Fig. 1) and cut using miter saw. ***Note:*** *Rabbeted edge should be on inside, or short side, of cut.*

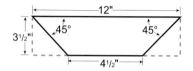

Family of Frames
Fig. 1
Cut ends of 1x4 at 45° angles

ASSEMBLE

1 Run a bead of glue down the center of each mitered edge and smooth with paint brush or piece of cardboard.

Press edges together and secure with adjustable corner clamp. Let dry. ***Note:*** *It is important to place all sides together at one time and clamp the entire piece. If a cut is off even ⅛ of a degree, that will total 1 degree because 8 cuts are made. Clamping the entire frame ensures even compensation for any imperfections.*

2 Remove corner clamp. Clamp frame to a flat surface and secure by either of the following two methods:

Nailing—Predrill a hole in each corner of frame and secure with finish nails. Set nails.

Dowels—Using dowel jig, drill holes through corresponding guides in the jig; glue dowels in holes (Fig. 2).

3 Fill holes with wood putty; let dry. Sand surfaces smooth and remove dust.

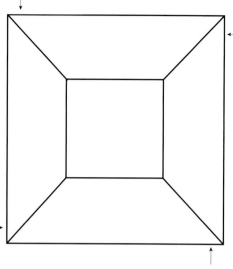

Family of Frames
Fig. 2
Using dowel jig, drill holes and insert dowels

PROJECT SIZE

11½x11½x¾ inches

TOOLS

- Table saw
- Miter saw
- Adjustable corner clamp
- Drill
- Dowel jig and wooden dowels (optional)
- Nail set

SUPPLIES FOR ONE FRAME

- 1x4 pine*: 6 feet
- Wood glue
- 1½-inch 6d finish nails
- Fine-grit sandpaper
- Wood putty

Select wood with a smooth grain, free of knots and imperfections. Make sure wood is not warped.

For Mystique Frame
- Krylon Mystique magenta/gold kit #1442

For Sparkling Sand Frame
- DecoArt sandstones golden fleck #DSD21 stonelike textural acrylic finish
- Soft brush or roller
- Matte spray varnish
- Assorted seashells
- Crafter's Pick The Ultimate! glue from API

For Beach House Frame
- DecoArt Americana colonial green #DA81 acrylic paint
- DecoArt Staining/Antiquing medium
- Soft brush and cloth
- Molding

- Crafter's Pick The Ultimate! glue from API
- Painter's tape
- Matte spray varnish

For Wood-Grained Frame
- Prestain wood conditioner
- Soft brush or lint-free cloths
- Walnut stain
- Krylon matte UV Protectant finish

For Fleur de Lis Frame
- Krylon Home Décor white primer #7438 spray acrylic paint
- DecoArt Glazing Medium
- DecoArt Americana acrylic paint: light mocha #DA241 and French mocha #DA188
- Paintbrushes
- DecoArt Perfect Crackle two-step crackle medium

Finishes

MYSTIQUE FRAME

Note: *Follow manufacturer's directions throughout for mixing and applying finish in each step.*

1 Apply two or three thin coats of base-coat black until even coverage is achieved. Let dry at least 30 minutes.

2 Apply three to six coats of magenta/gold until desired color is achieved, allowing to become tacky between coats.

3 Apply two to three coats of top coat, allowing to become tacky or dry between coats. Let dry one hour.

SPARKLING SAND FRAME

1 Following manufacturer's directions, apply a generous coat

- Soft cloth
- Thick craft foam
- Craft knife
- Painter's tape
- DecoArt natural #AST02 Americana Stuccos
- Spatula
- Matte varnish

For Stained Glass Frame
- Pencil and paper
- Waxed paper
- Paper cups
- DecoArt Magic Medium
- DecoArt Americana acrylic paint: red violet #DA140
- DecoArt Dazzling Metallics: crystal green #DA076, ice blue #DA075, purple pearl #DA124, Venetian gold #DA072 and white pearl #DA117

- Jumbo craft sticks
- Krylon Home Décor white primer #7438 spray acrylic paint
- Painter's Tape
- DecoArt Glazing Medium
- Paintbrushes
- Plastic bag
- DecoArt Magic Medium leading
- Matte varnish

For Cherry Veneer Frame
- ¾-inch cherry veneer edging
- Household iron
- Veneer roller or wood block
- Craft knife or razor blade
- Metal straight edge
- 8x32-inch sheet cherry veneer
- Painter's tape
- Brush
- Fast-drying contact cement

- Woodsheen wipe-on gel stain and finish by Minwax
- Soft cloth

For Maple Burl & Birch Veneer Frame
- ¾-inch birch veneer edging
- 2-inch birch veneer edging
- Household iron
- Veneer roller or wood block
- Craft knife or razor blade
- Metal straight edge
- 8x32-inch maple burl veneer
- Painter's tape
- Brush
- Fast-drying contact cement
- Woodsheen wipe-on gel stain and finish by Minwax
- Soft cloth

of sandstone finish with a soft brush or roller; let dry.

2 Apply a second coat in a crosshatch manner; let dry.

3 Spray with matte varnish for added durability; let dry.

4 Use The Ultimate! glue to attach seashells to front of frame as desired.

BEACH HOUSE FRAME

1 Mix equal amounts of Staining/ Antiquing medium and colonial green. Apply to front and edges of frame using a soft brush, then wipe

off excess with a soft cloth to give a weathered appearance. Repeat process to achieve desired effect.

2 Determine where you want to put molding on frame. Measure the length of the outside of that square and use as a guide for cutting all four pieces. ***Note:*** *If molding has a pattern, make sure to begin each cut so patterns will line up.*

3 Position molding around frame opening. Mark outer edge of molding with painter's tape; remove molding. Use a brush to apply The Ultimate! glue to backs of molding pieces; brush a thin line along inside

of painter's tape. Allow glue to become clear, then press molding into place. Remove painter's tape. Let dry.

4 Spray frame with matte varnish; let dry.

WOOD-GRAINED FRAME

1 Following manufacturer's directions, apply wood conditioner to frame with a soft brush or lint-free cloth; let set 5–15 minutes, then remove excess with a clean, dry cloth.

2 Using a soft brush or lint-free cloth, apply stain and wipe off excess following manufacturer's directions. Repeat to achieve desired shade. Let dry.

3 Spray frame with several thin coats of matte UV Protectant finish. Let dry at least 30 minutes.

FLEUR DE LIS FRAME

1 Following manufacturer's directions, apply two to three coats of white primer to frame to cover evenly. Let dry 30 minutes.

2 Mix one part light mocha with two parts glazing medium. Using paintbrush, apply a thin coat of glazing mixture to entire surface of frame to create a mottled effect. Let dry completely.

3 With a soft brush, apply a thick coat of step 1 of Perfect Crackle two-step crackle medium; let dry. Apply a second coat for larger cracks; let dry.

4 Apply French mocha with a soft brush and lightly wipe off with a soft cloth; let dry.

5 Using pattern provided (page 41) and craft knife, cut fleur de lis stencil from craft foam. Position foam stencil on frame and tape in place. Using spatula, fill with stucco, then carefully lift off foam. **Note:** *The thicker the stucco is applied, the more cracks will form when drying.* Let dry 72 hours.

6 Spray with matte varnish.

STAINED GLASS FRAME

1 Draw six 1x8-inch rectangles on paper, spacing ¾ to 1 inch apart; place paper under waxed paper.

2 Pour equal amounts of Magic Medium into six paper cups. To each cup, add 3 to 5 drops of one

color acrylic paint and swirl three times with a jumbo craft stick. Pour contents of cups over waxed paper, covering each strip area with one color; spread each color to ⅛-inch thickness using craft stick. **Note:** *Move cup in a circular or zigzag motion when pouring to create pattern.* Let dry 24 to 48 hours.

3 Following manufacturer's directions, apply two or three thin coats of white primer to frame to achieve even coverage. Let dry 30 minutes.

4 With painter's tape, mask off a ¾-inch-wide border around frame opening. In a paper cup, mix one part white pearl and two parts glazing medium, then add a dab of Venetian gold. With paintbrush, apply mixture to frame's surface. While still wet, dab off with a crumpled plastic bag to create a mottled appearance. Let dry completely. Remove painter's tape.

5 Peel dry medium from waxed paper and cut into 1x8-inch strips. Cut strips into shapes; arrange shapes around outer edge of ¾-inch border around frame opening, spacing ⅛ inch apart. Glue in place using Magic Medium glue.

6 Apply Magic Medium leading following manufacturer's directions; let dry.

7 Paint border inside stained glass border with Venetian gold; let dry.

8 Spray with matte varnish; let dry.

CHERRY VENEER FRAME
Photo of this frame appears on page 35.

1 **Note:** *Measure and cut each strip of veneer one at a time.* On outer edge, measure one side of frame; cut one strip of ¾-inch cherry veneer edging ½-inch longer than

measurement. Set iron to cotton setting; position edging and slowly press iron over length of veneer. While still hot, press veneer down firmly using veneer roller or wood block. If veneer is positioned incorrectly, reheat and reposition. Trim excess, if needed, using craft knife or razor blade. Repeat to cover all four sides.

2 Repeat step 1 on inner edge of frame, cutting each strip of veneer the same length as measurement.

3 Mark vertical center of frame with a pencil line. Place frame on veneer sheet, aligning edge with center line, and trace frame onto veneer sheet. Mark wrong side of piece "A." Repeat for opposite side of frame, and mark veneer "B."

4 Cut out pattern using metal straight edge and craft knife. **Note:** *Score your cut. Do not press too hard or you may tear the veneer. Run the knife along the score several times until it cuts through.*

5 Lay veneer on frame to check for accuracy; remove veneer. Cover edges of frame with painter's tape, then liberally apply glue to surface of frame and wrong side of veneer using a brush; allow to become tacky. Place wooden dowels across top and bottom of frame, then lay veneer A on top of dowels. Align veneer carefully with edges of frame, then carefully remove dowels one at a time and press veneer onto frame. Repeat with veneer B. Press veneer firmly into place using veneer roller or wooden block, forcing out air bubbles.

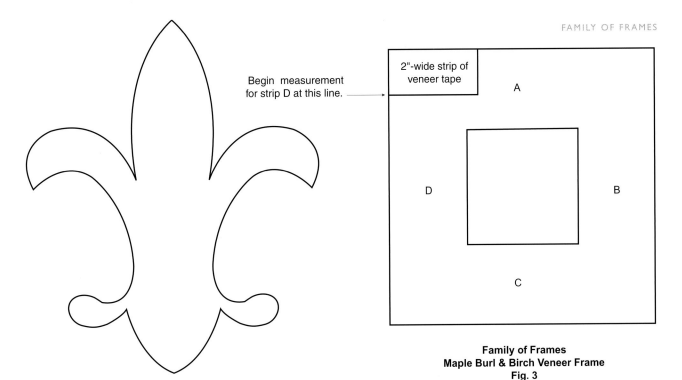

Family of Frames
Fleur de Lis

Family of Frames
Maple Burl & Birch Veneer Frame
Fig. 3

6 Apply gel stain and finish with a soft cloth; allow to penetrate 20 minutes, then wipe off excess. Repeat to achieve desired shade.

MAPLE BURL & BIRCH VENEER FRAME

Photo of this frame appears on page 35.

1 *Note: Measure and cut each strip of veneer one at a time.* On outer edge, measure one side of frame; cut one strip of ¾-inch birch veneer edging ½-inch longer than measurement. Set iron to cotton setting; position edging and slowly press iron over length of veneer. While still hot, press veneer down firmly using veneer roller or wood block. If veneer is positioned incorrectly, reheat and reposition. Trim excess, if needed, using craft knife or razor blade. Repeat to cover all four sides.

2 Repeat step 1 on inner edge of frame, cutting each strip of veneer the same length as measurement.

Family of Frames
Maple Burl & Birch Veneer Frame
Fig. 4

3 With a pencil, lightly mark the front of the frame with A, B, C and D (Fig. 3). Cut a 4-inch long strip of 2-inch-wide birch veneer edging and tape in place on frame as illustrated.

4 Measure D side of frame from bottom of strip to edge of frame and cut another strip of 2-inch-wide

veneer edging ½ inch longer than measurement (Fig. 4). Set iron to cotton setting. Position edging along edge of frame and slowly press into place with iron. While still warm, press veneer down firmly using veneer roller or wood block. If positioned incorrectly, reheat and reposition. Trim excess with craft knife. Repeat process for C side, B

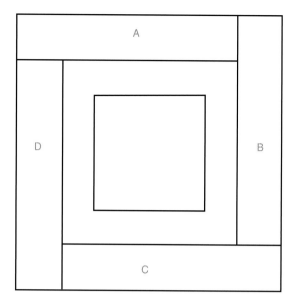

Family of Frames
Maple Burl & Birch Veneer Frame
Fig. 5

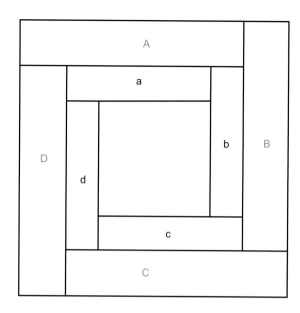

Family of Frames
Maple Burl & Birch Veneer Frame
Fig. 6

side and A side (Fig. 5). ***Note: Remove taped strip to complete A side.***

5 Measure frame from inside edge of birch veneer to inside edge of frame. Cut maple burl veneer in strips this width to cover remaining area on frame, marking each remaining side of frame as before, a, b, c and d (Fig. 6); measure and cut the length of each strip one strip at a time.

6 Cover birch veneer edging with painter's tape. Use a brush to apply glue liberally to the surface of the frame and the wrong side of the maple burl veneer; allow to become tacky. Carefully position veneer strips, then press into place. Press firmly with veneer roller or wood block, forcing out air bubbles.

7 Apply gel stain and finish with a soft cloth; allow to penetrate 20 minutes, then wipe off excess. Repeat to achieve desired shade. ❁

MYSTIC FRAME

27 **TWO-COLOR DAZZLE** Krylon's Mystique kit creates a dazzling illusion of two colors moving and shifting on one surface. The easy three-step application dries fast. The kit includes everything you need in one convenient package.

SPARKLING SAND FRAME

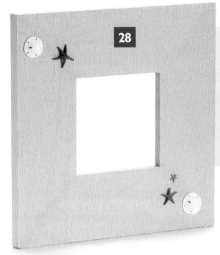

28 SPARKLING SAND

Create the look of real granite on indoor and outdoor projects with one-step DecoArt Sandstone textural paint. It's easier and less expensive than similar spray paint, is weatherproof, dries to the touch in 10 minutes and cleans up with soap and water.

BEACH HOUSE FRAME

29 STAINING AND ANTIQUING

Mix any acrylic paint with DecoArt Staining/Antiquing medium and apply to wood as a stain for soft, translucent color. It is nontoxic and easy to clean up with soap and water.

30 PURCHASED MOLDING

Wood molding is mitered at the corners and glued to the front of the frame for a decorative finish.

12 CLEAR UV PROTECTANT

This tough spray-on finish by Krylon is moisture- and chip-resistant and dries to a durable protective coating in minutes. The nonyellowing formula provides protection against harmful ultraviolet light.

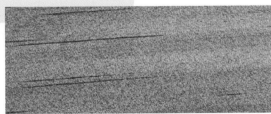

WOOD-GRAINED FRAME

FLEUR DE LIS FRAME

31 CRACKLE PAINT

DecoArt's two-step crackle medium dries clear and can be antiqued for an aged look. Apply light, even coats for tiny cracks, or two to three heavy coats for large cracks.

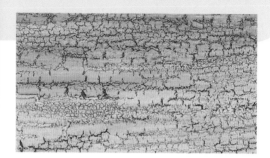

32 MAKE YOUR OWN STENCIL

A homemade stencil and Americana Stuccos from DecoArt are all you need to create an elegant embossed pattern on this frame. Simply smooth a layer of Stuccos over the stencil and lift—the stucco will retain the stencil's shape as it dries.

CHERRY VENEER FRAME

33 SIMPLY VENEER

Create the look of exotic or expensive wood with veneers, which can be trimmed to size with a craft knife. Iron-on veneer edge tape makes it easy to do.

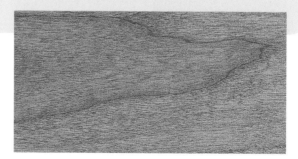

STAINED GLASS FRAME

34 STAINED GLASS PAINT

Mix a few drops of any acrylic paint with Magic Medium by DecoArt to create the look of stained glass on any project. Just mix, pour and let dry, then cut with a craft knife and adhere to your project.

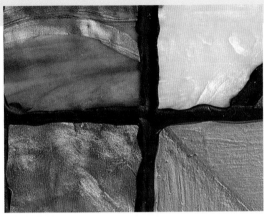

35 CRUMPLED PLASTIC BAG MOTTLED FINISH

Use a crumpled plastic bag to dab wet paint off the surface of a frame, creating a mottled finish.

MAPLE BURL & BIRCH VENEER FRAME

36 TWO-TONE VENEER

Different varieties of wood veneer create an interesting pattern on a large, flat surface. Use contact cement to adhere the veneer to the plain pine frame.

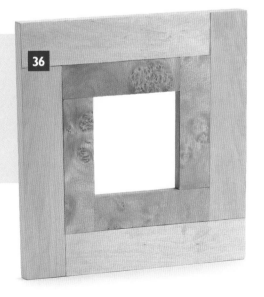

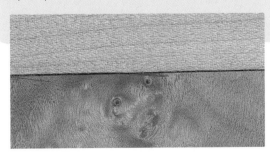

FUN
PHOTO FRAMES

Designs by Loretta Mateik

Creative finishes turn these simple frames into works of art worthy of displaying your treasured memories.

CUTTING

1 Enlarge frame pattern 117 percent. Use graphite paper to transfer enlarged pattern onto pine; cut out 8-inch square using band saw, then round corners using scroll saw.

2 Drill a ½-inch hole in center of frame for starter hole, then cut out center opening with scroll saw.

3 Drill a 5⁄64-inch hole for inserting wooden dowel in center-bottom of frame back, ¾ inch from bottom.

4 Using router with ⅜-inch rabbeting bit, rout a ¼-inch-deep rabbet around opening edge on back of frame.

5 Sand frame smooth and remove dust.

ASSEMBLE

1 Cut photo and cardboard to fit and place in opening; secure with one framing point on each edge.

2 Glue wooden dowel in hole on back for frame stand.

Finishes

SLIP-SLAP FRAME

1 Base-coat front and back of frame and wooden dowel with white; let dry. Sand lightly and remove dust. Apply a coat of yellow over white on frame; paint wooden dowel with tangerine. Let dry.

2 Using comb brush and tangerine, randomly apply slip-slap strokes to front of frame. Let dry.

3 Following manufacturer's directions, apply several light coats of matte varnish to entire frame.

MARBLED FRAME

1 Using 1-inch glaze/wash brush, base-coat front and back of frame and wooden dowel with black; let dry. Sand lightly and remove dust. Apply a second coat; let dry.

2 Mix 10 parts clear glazing medium with three parts gold metallic paint. Cut a piece of plastic wrap larger than the frame. Apply glaze/gold mixture to front of frame.

PROJECT SIZE
8x8x¾ inches

TOOLS
- Band saw
- Scroll saw
- Router with ⅜-inch rabbeting bit
- Drill with 5⁄64- and ½-inch bits

For Friends Frame
- Small palette knife

SUPPLIES FOR ONE FRAME
- ¾x8x8-inch pine*
- Sandpaper
- Graphite paper
- Masking tape
- 2 inches ⅜-inch wooden dowel
- Cardboard
- Four ⅝-inch framing points
- Matte spray varnish

Measurements given are actual, not nominal. Standard nominal lumber will need to be ripped to size.

For Slip-Slap Frame
- Ceramcoat acrylic paint from Delta: white #2505, yellow #2504 and tangerine #2043
- Paintbrushes: 1-inch glaze/wash and ½-inch comb

For Marbled Frame
- 1-inch glaze/wash paintbrush
- Ceramcoat black #2506 acrylic paint from Delta
- Jo Sonja's clear glazing medium
- Ceramcoat Sheer Metallics gold acrylic paint from Delta
- Plastic wrap

For Friends Frame
- Ceramcoat acrylic paint from Delta: Bahama purple #2518 and vintage wine #2434
- 1-inch glaze/wash paintbrush
- Stencil adhesive
- Simply Stencils Laser sentiments #28250 stencil from Plaid
- Decorating Paste from DecoArt

SLIP-SLAP FRAME

37 SLIP-SLAP TECHNIQUE

Use a stiff comb brush to "slap" contrasting paint in a random pattern to create this fun frame. Kids and teens will enjoy personalizing their spaces with different paint combinations.

MARBLED FRAME

38 METALLIC MARBLED

Create a marbled look by squishing plastic wrap with your fingers. If you don't like the results, you can just wipe off the wet glaze mixture and repeat. It's fun and easy to do.

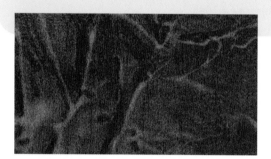

FRIENDS FRAME

39 DECORATING PASTE

This semitransparent product by DecoArt dries to a firm, yet slightly flexible, textural surface that won't crack or peel off. It can be tinted with acrylic paint before application or painted when dry. It is nontoxic and cleans up with soap and water.

3 Working quickly, lay plastic wrap on frame and squish the wrap with your fingers, forming folds and creases to cover front of frame. Grasp two opposite sides of wrap and, with one gentle but constant motion, pull off the plastic wrap. ***Note:** If dissatisfied with the results, wipe with a damp paper towel and repeat.* Let dry.

4 Apply glaze/gold mixture to back of frame and repeat step 3.

5 Apply glaze/gold mixture to one side of frame, then dab with a crumpled ball of plastic wrap. Let dry. Repeat on remaining three sides.

6 Following manufacturer's directions, apply several light coats of matte varnish to entire frame.

FRIENDS FRAME

1 Mix a drop or two of vintage wine into Bahama purple; paint both sides of frame and wooden dowel. Let dry. Sand smooth and remove dust. Apply a second coat; let dry.

2 Cut "Friends" and decorative flower border from stencil. Spray back of "Friends" with adhesive and center along bottom edge of center opening. Apply masking tape around all edges of cut stencil.

3 Using palette knife, trowel decorating paste over stencil openings, picking up enough paste to cover stencil in one smooth pass. Carefully lift off stencil.

4 Position flower border on one side of opening; repeat step 3. Reposition flower border stencil on opposite side of opening and repeat again. Let dry, then reposition flower border across top of opening and apply paste.

5 Referring to photo for placement, apply an individual curlicue from flower border stencil on each side of "Friends" at bottom of frame opening. Let dry.

6 Following manufacturer's directions, apply several light coats of matte varnish to entire frame. ❈

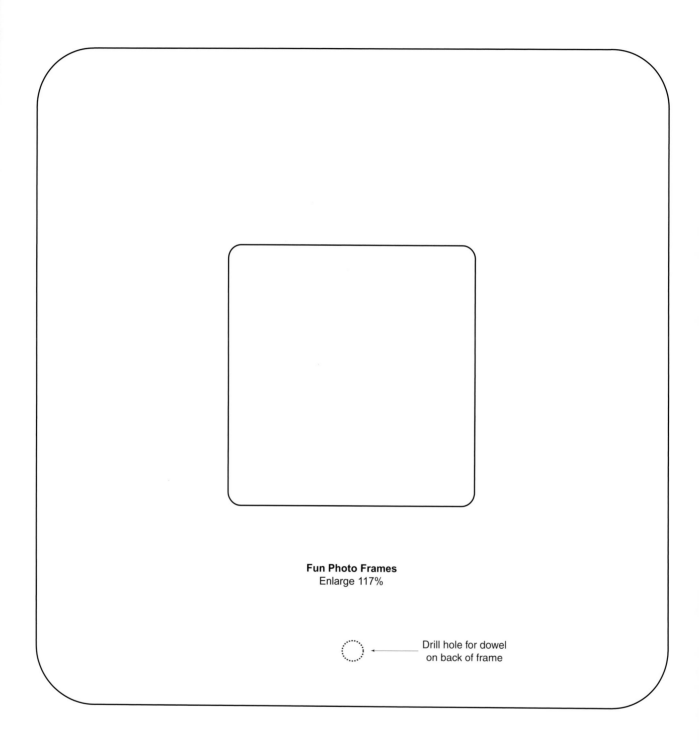

Fun Photo Frames
Enlarge 117%

Drill hole for dowel
on back of frame

BANK OF
DRAWERS

Designs by Anna Thompson

Organize every room in your house with an easy-to-build box filled with drawers. Basic joinery and simple hardwood drawer runners make this the perfect piece to fill with crafting supplies, kids' toys or out-of-season clothing.

PROJECT NOTE

Most lumber suppliers will cut plywood to size for a small fee. If this service is not available, use cordless circular saw to cut dimensions given in instructions.

CUTTING

1 From ¾-inch plywood, cut two 14¼x30½-inch pieces (A) for case sides, two 14¼x23¹⁄₁₆-inch pieces (B) for case bottom and case auxiliary top, and one 14¾x24½-inch piece (Q) for top.

2 Using router and ¼-inch bit, cut a rabbet along back edge of case sides (A) and case bottom and case auxiliary top (B).

3 From ½-inch plywood, cut 8-foot lengths as follows: three 5½-inch widths, one 5-inch width and one 4-inch width. Using table saw, cut a ¼-inch-wide groove ½-inch from one long edge of each 8-foot length. From remaining ½-inch plywood, cut three 6⅛x23¹⁄₁₆-inch pieces (N) for drawer Nos. 3, 4 and 5 fronts, one 5⅝x23⅙-inch piece (O) for Drawer No. 2 front, and one 4½x23¹⁄₁₆-inch piece (P) for drawer No. 1 front (Fig. 1).

4 From ½x5½-inch grooved lengths, cut six 22-inch lengths (G) for drawer Nos. 3, 4 and 5 backs and auxiliary fronts, and six 14-inch lengths (H) for drawer Nos. 3, 4 and 5 sides.

5 From ½x5-inch grooved length, cut two 22-inch lengths (I) for drawer No. 2 back and auxiliary front, and two 14-inch lengths (J) for drawer No. 2 sides.

6 From ½x4-inch-wide grooved length, cut two 22-inch lengths (K) for drawer No. 1 back and auxiliary

PROJECT SIZE

25½x31¼x15¼ inches

TOOLS

- Cordless circular saw (optional)
- Miter saw
- Table saw
- Router with ¼-inch straight bit
- Drill

SUPPLIES

- ¾-inch birch plywood: 4x8-feet and 4x4-feet
- ½-inch birch plywood: 4x8-feet
- ¼-inch birch plywood: 4x4-feet
- ½x¾-inch birch*: two 8-foot lengths
- ¾x⅝-inch birch*: 8 feet
- ¾x⅞-inch birch*: 3 feet
- Wood glue
- 2-inch wood screws
- 1¾-inch wood screws
- 1¼-inch brads
- Ten 1¼-inch wooden knobs with screws
- ¾-inch wood screws
- ⅜-inch wood plugs
- Double-sided carpet tape

**Measurements given are actual, not nominal. Standard nominal lumber will need to be ripped to size.*

For Classic Cherry Drawers

- Soft, lint-free cloth
- Wood Kote cherry Jel'd Stain
- Wood Kote Jel'd Poly Kote

For Easy Birch Drawers

- Soft, lint-free cloth
- Wood Kote Jel'd Poly Kote

For Colorful Kids' Drawers

- Krylon Interior/Exterior spray primer
- Krylon Interior/Exterior spray paint: Dover white #3555 and desired colors
- Krylon green #0806 Chalkboard spray paint
- Krylon Magnetic paint #3151
- Krylon Glowz #3150 glow-in-the-dark paint
- Krylon magical multicolor #405 Glitter Spray
- Krylon yellow #KDH5241 Fluorescent paint

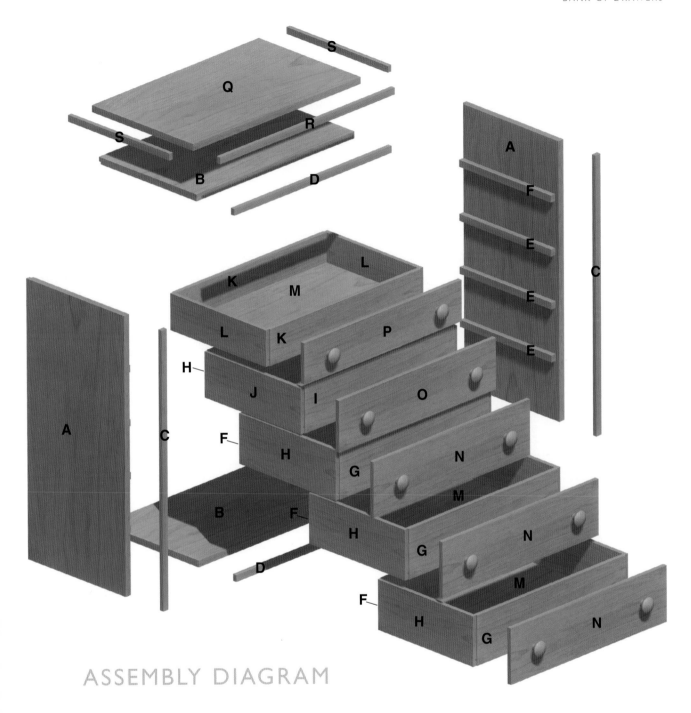

ASSEMBLY DIAGRAM

BANK OF DRAWERS CUTTING CHART (Actual Sizes)				
P	T	W	L	#
A	¾"	14¼"	30½"	2
B	¾"	14¼"	23¹/₁₆"	2
C	½"	¾"	30½"	2
D	½"	¾"	23"	2
E	¾"	⅝"	13½"	6

F	¾"	⅞"	13½"	2
G	½"	5½"	22"	6
H	½"	5½"	14"	6
I	½"	5"	22"	2
J	½"	5"	14"	2
K	½"	4"	22"	2
L	½"	4"	14"	2

M	¼"	13¾"	22½"	5
N	½"	6⅛"	23¹/₁₆"	3
O	½"	5⅝"	23¹/₁₆"	1
P	½"	4½"	23¹/₁₆"	1
Q	¾"	14¾"	24½"	1
R	½"	¾"	25½"	1
S	½"	¾"	14¾"	2

CLASSIC CHERRY DRAWERS

40 SEMITRANSPARENT WOOD STAIN

This industrial-strength finish by Wood Kote is a semitransparent wood stain formulated for hand application. Use Jel'd Kote in a well-ventilated area and be sure to add a few coats of polyurethane or varnish to protect the wood.

front, and two 14-inch lengths (L) for drawer No. 1 sides.

7 From ¼-inch plywood cut five 13¾x22½-inch pieces (M) for drawer bottoms.

8 From ½x¾-inch birch, cut two 30½-inch lengths (C) for case front side edgings, two 23-inch lengths (D) for case front top/bottom edgings, one 25½-inch length (R) for case top front edging, and two 14¾-inch lengths (S) for case top side edgings.

9 From ¾x⅝-inch birch, cut six 13½-inch lengths (E) for drawer Nos. 2,

3 and 4 runners. From ¾x⅞-inch birch, cut two 13½-inch lengths (F) for drawer No. 1 runners.

ASSEMBLE

1 Assemble case sides (A), case bottom (B) and case auxiliary top (B) with 2-inch screws and glue, making sure front edges are flush. ***Note:*** *Predrill and countersink for ⅜-inch flush wood plugs.*

2 Glue and nail case front edging pieces (C, D) to front edges of case. ***Note:*** *Predrill before attaching brads to prevent splitting.*

3 Referring to Fig. 2, glue drawer runners (E, F) inside case, then screw in place using 1¼-inch screws.

4 Assemble drawer Nos. 3, 4 and 5 backs/auxiliary fronts (G), sides (H) and bottom (M); secure with glue and brads. Repeat with drawer No. 2 (I, J, M) and drawer No. 1 (K, L, M).

5 Position drawer fronts (N, O, P) on corresponding auxiliary drawer fronts and hold in place with double-sided carpet tape; drill for knobs. Attach knobs to secure fronts. Drill for and insert ¾-inch screws from inside drawers to further secure drawer fronts.

6 Attach top (Q) to case auxiliary top using 1¼-inch screws from inside case. Attach top front and top side edgings (R, S) using glue and brads. ***Note:*** *Predrill holes to prevent wood from splitting.*

```
|<------------- 22" ------------->|

| Drawer No. 1              4¹/₂" |
|                                 |
| Drawer No. 2              5⁵/₈" |
|                                 |
| Drawer No. 3              6¹/₈" |
|                                 |
| Drawer No. 4              6¹/₈" |
|                                 |
| Drawer No. 5              6¹/₈" |
```

Bank of Drawers
Front View
Fig. 1

EASY BIRCH DRAWERS

41 WIPE-ON POLY

This wipe-on polyurethane by Wood Kote is designed for use on interior surfaces that will not receive heavy use. Jel'd Poly Kote will yellow slightly over time and with exposure to light, so it should not be used over white or pastel finishes. It is easy to apply and dries fast to a hard, smooth, glossy finish.

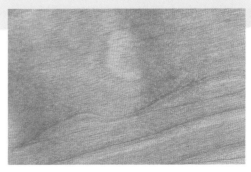

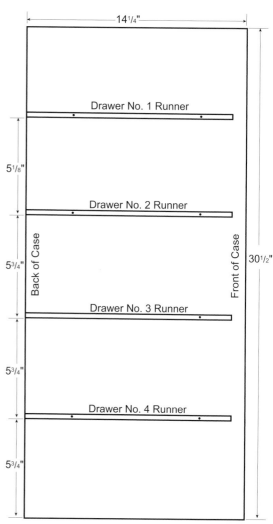

Dimensions shown on side view: 14¹⁄₄", 30¹⁄₂", 5¹⁄₈", 5³⁄₄", 5³⁄₄", 5³⁄₄"

Drawer No. 1 Runner
Drawer No. 2 Runner
Drawer No. 3 Runner
Drawer No. 4 Runner

Back of Case

Front of Case

**Bank of Drawers
Side View
Fig. 2**

7 Glue furniture plugs in place. Sand edges and surfaces of project smooth; remove dust.

Finishes

CLASSIC CHERRY DRAWERS

1 Following manufacturer's directions, apply two coats of Jel'd Stain, letting dry after each coat.

2 Apply three coats of Jel'd Poly Kote. **Note:** *If color is picked up on cloth when applying finish, stain is not dry yet and needs more time.*

EASY BIRCH DRAWERS

Following manufacturer's directions, apply three to four coats of Jel'd Stain, letting dry after each coat.

COLORFUL KIDS' DRAWERS

1 Apply two coats of primer to all exterior surfaces, letting dry and sanding lightly between coats.

2 **Notes:** *Remove knobs and paint separately, then reattach when finished.* Follow manufacturer's directions for applying all paints. Spray case with two coats of interior/

exterior paint. Finish each drawer as follows:

Drawer No. 1—Spray with magnetic paint.

Drawer No. 2—Spray with chalkboard paint.

Drawer No. 3—Base-coat with Dover white. Apply glow-in-the-dark paint over base coat.

Drawer No. 4—Spray with Glitter Spray.

Drawer No. 5—Base-coat with Dover white. Apply yellow fluorescent paint over base coat. ❈

42 SPRAY-ON ACRYLIC

Krylon's fast-drying interior/exterior spray paint goes on evenly to create a smooth, long-lasting finish. It dries in 12 minutes or less, so you can get the look you want in no time!

43 MAGNETIC PAINT

This primer finish by Krylon can be top coated with any paint color to create a magnetic surface in kids' rooms, classrooms, workshops, kitchens and more.

COLORFUL KIDS' DRAWERS

44 CHALKBOARD PAINT

Create a tough, slatelike surface that's durable and functional. This Krylon spray product is easy to apply.

45 GLOWZ

Make your project stand out with this glow-in-the-dark spray or brush-on product from Krylon. It produces a glowing effect and recharges with exposure to light. Use over a white base coat for best results.

47 FLUORESCENT PAINT

Neon colors glow under an ultraviolet (black) light so popular with teens. Use over a white base coat for best results.

46 GLITTER SPRAY

Add a shimmering finish to this drawer front with this spray-on product from Krylon. No mess and nonclogging formula make it easy to use.

VERSATILE BEADBOARD CABINETS

Designs by Anna Thompson

Equally at home in the living room, play room, bedroom or front porch, this small storage cabinet features beadboard on the end panels and doors.

CUTTING FOR CABINET

1 From ¾x2-inch poplar, cut eight 21-inch lengths (A) for four front and back stiles and four rails, and four 9-inch lengths (C) for end rails.

2 From ¾x1¼-inch poplar, cut four 21-inch lengths (B) for end stiles.

3 Referring to Fig. 1, cut one end of each stile as shown.

4 From beadboard panel, cut one 22x14-inch piece (D) for back, and two 10x14-inch pieces (E) for ends.

5 From ½-inch plywood, cut one 11½x23⅝-inch piece (H) for bottom.

6 For antique walnut and rich red cabinet, cut one 14x26⅝-inch piece (I) for top from ¾-inch plywood. For sleek black cabinet, cut ¾x14-inch cherry to 26⅝-inch length (I) for top.

7 From ¾x¾-inch stock, cut four 23½-inch lengths (F) for front and back cleats, and four 10-inch lengths (G) for end cleats.

ASSEMBLE CABINET

Note: Predrill for screws using ⅛-inch bit, and countersink using ⅜-inch forstner bit.

1 Referring to Fig. 2, lay out stiles (A, B) and rails (A, C) for front, back and ends; mark placement of joints,

PROJECT SIZE
26⅝x21¾x14 inches

TOOLS
- Table saw
- Miter saw
- Doweling jig
- Clamps
- Router with ⅜-inch rabbet bit
- Drill with ⅛-inch bit and ⅜-inch forstner bit

SUPPLIES FOR ONE CABINET
- ¾x2-inch poplar*: two 8-foot lengths and one 4-foot length
- ¾x1¼-inch poplar*: one 8-foot length
- 1x2 poplar: one 8-foot length
- ⅜-inch beadboard panel: 4x4 feet
- ½-inch birch plywood: 2x4 feet
- ¾-inch birch plywood: 2x4 feet (for antique walnut or rich red cabinet)
- ¾x14-inch* edge-glued cherry panel: 3 feet (for sleek black cabinet)
- ¾x¾-inch* stock: 12 feet
- Forty-eight ⁵⁄₁₆-inch dowel pins
- Sandpaper: 80- to 220-grit
- ¾-inch wood screws
- 1¼-inch wood screws
- ¾-inch birch iron-on edge tape (for antique walnut or rich red cabinet)
- Household iron
- ⅜-inch wood plugs
- Four 1½-inch hinges
- Two 1½-inch wooden knobs with screws
- Paint roller and pan
- Lint-free disposable cloths

Measurement given is actual, not nominal. Standard nominal lumber will need to be ripped to size.

For Antique Walnut Cabinet
- Medium walnut Danish Oil Finish by Deft
- Foam brushes
- Fast-drying semigloss Clear Wood Finish by Deft

For Sleek Black Cabinet
- Krylon glossy black #1601 Interior/Exterior paint
- Natural Deftoil Danish Oil by Deft

For Rich Red Cabinet
- Medium walnut Danish Oil Finish by Deft
- Foam brushes
- Cranberry color semigloss wall paint
- Fast-drying semigloss Clear Wood Finish by Deft

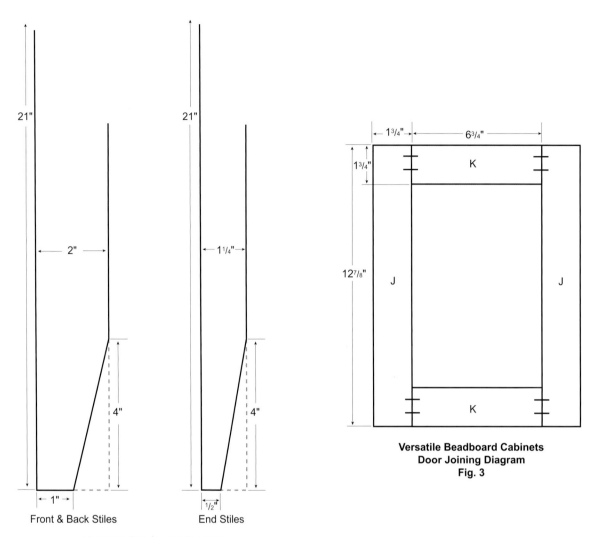

21"

2"

4"

1"

Front & Back Stiles

21"

1¼"

4"

½"

End Stiles

Versatile Beadboard Cabinets
Fig. 1

1¾"   6¾"

1¾"

K

12⅞"   J   J

K

Versatile Beadboard Cabinets
Door Joining Diagram
Fig. 3

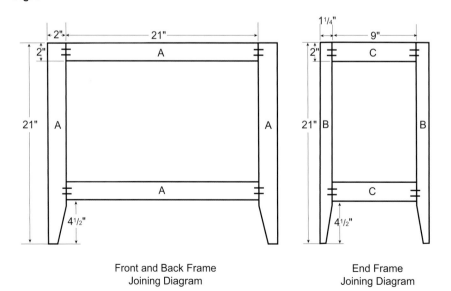

2"   21"

2"   A

21"   A   A

A

4½"

Front and Back Frame
Joining Diagram

1¼"

9"

2"   C

21"   B   B

C

4½"

End Frame
Joining Diagram

Versatile Beadboard Cabinets
Fig. 2

ASSEMBLY DIAGRAM

VERSATILE BEADBOARD CABINETS CUTTING CHART (Actual Sizes)				
P	T	W	L	#
A	¾"	2"	21"	8
B	¾"	1¼"	21"	4
C	¾"	2"	9"	4
D	⅜"	22"	14"	1
E	⅜"	10"	14"	2
F	¾"	¾"	23½"	4
G	¾"	¾"	10"	4
H	½"	11½"	23⅝"	1
I	¾"	14"	26⅝"	1
J	¾"	1½"	12⅞"	4
K	¾"	1½"	6¾"	4
L	⅜"	7½"	10¼"	2

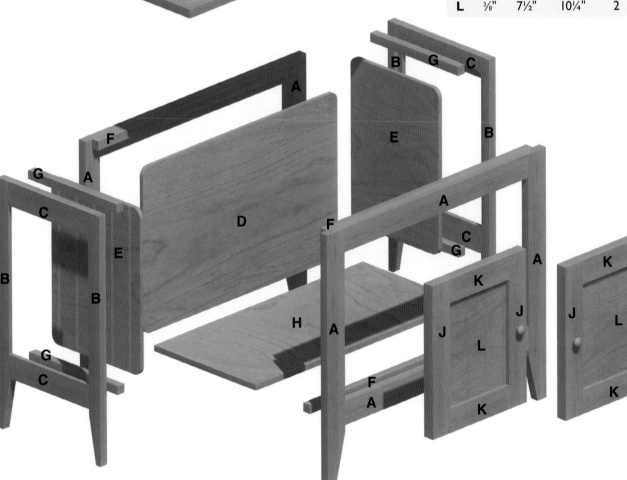

1 DANISH OIL
Using a foam brush, apply more oil to the lighter areas of the wood to even out the natural variations in color that occur in some woods.

1 DANISH OIL
Flood the surface using a paint roller drenched in oil, keep the surface wet for 30 minutes, and then wipe off all the excess and allow to dry. This penetrating finish seals from the inside out, rather than lying on the surface.

4 SEMIGLOSS LACQUER
This Deft product can be applied with a brush or sprayed on for a baby-safe, fast-drying, crystal-clear finish on furniture, cabinets, paneling, antiques and crafts.

ANTIQUE WALNUT CABINET

then drill for dowels. Dry-fit, then glue and clamp. Let dry. Sand edges flush.

2 Rout a ⅜-inch rabbet around the inside of each frame. ***Note:** Rout in clockwise direction, taking several light passes to avoid tearout.*

3 Round corners of beadboard (D, E) to fit inside rabbets. Attach beadboard to frames using ¾-inch screws, taking care not to go through the front of the frame.

4 Referring to assembly diagram, attach front and back to sides using 1¼-inch screws. Attach front, back and end cleats (F, G) around top and bottom edges using 1¼-inch screws. Attach bottom (H) to bottom cleats using ¾-inch screws.

5 For antique walnut and rich red cabinet, apply iron-on edge tape to edges of top (I) using household iron; sand edges flush. Center top on cabinet and attach with ¾-inch screws through top cleats. *Note: For sleek black cabinet, do not attach cherry top (I) until pieces are finished.*

6 Glue wood plugs in screw holes; let dry. Using 150-grit sandpaper, sand all edges and surfaces smooth, taking care to sand beadboard panels; remove dust.

CUTTING FOR DOORS
Note: Dimensions on cutting chart are those for model project. For precise fit, measure and cut pieces as instructed below.

1 Measure height of front opening. From 1x2 poplar, cut four lengths ⅛-inch shorter than height of opening for door stiles (J).

2 To calculate length of door rails, measure width of front opening, then subtract ⅛ inch and the combined width of four stiles; divide in half. From 1x2 poplar, cut four lengths to this measurement for door rails (K).

ASSEMBLE DOORS

1 Lay out door stiles and rails; mark placement of joints, then drill for dowels (Fig. 3). Dry-fit, then glue and clamp. Let dry.

2 Rout inside edges of door frames as for cabinet frames. Cut two pieces of beadboard (L) to fit inside rabbets, rounding corners as for cabinet panels. Attach to door frames using ¾-inch

screws, taking care not to go through front of frame.

3 Using 150-grit sandpaper, sand all edges and surfaces smooth, taking care to sand beadboard panels; remove dust.

4 Attach doors to cabinet with hinges. Attach knobs to doors.

Finishes
ANTIQUE WALNUT CABINET

1 Following manufacturer's directions, flood surface with

medium walnut Danish oil finish, using a paint roller drenched in the oil. Keep wet for 30 minutes, applying oil wherever the surface appears to be dry.

2 Wipe off excess oil. Let dry 2 hours.

3 Use a foam brush to even out color by applying additional oil to lighter areas. Let dry as before.

4 Apply three coats of fast-drying clear wood finish, sanding very lightly between coats with 220-grit sandpaper.

1 DANISH OIL

Make sure to finish the undersides of table and cabinet top to protect the wood and keep it stable. If you put several coats of oil on only one side, it could begin to cup and warp.

48 BLACK GLOSS PAINT

Black gloss paint, sprayed on in several thin layers, creates a deep, rich finish.

SLEEK BLACK CABINET

1 DANISH OIL

If the oil finish does not seem to dry and remains tacky even after several hours, it means the excess oil was not completely wiped off. If this happens, simply flood the surface with more oil to "melt" the tacky oil, and wipe down well.

RICH RED CABINET

SLEEK BLACK CABINET

1 Spray cabinet with several coats of glossy black paint following manufacturer's directions.

2 Beginning with 80-grit and ending with 220-grit, sand cherry top, making sure there are not machine marks left in wood and glue joints are not noticeable. Remove dust.

3 Following manufacturer's directions, apply four coats of Danish oil to cherry top as in steps 1 and 2 of antique walnut cabinet.

Note: *Finish both sides of the top to prevent wood from warping.*

4 Center top on cabinet and attach with 1¼-inch screws through top cleats.

RICH RED CABINET

1 Apply medium walnut Danish oil finish to cabinet as in steps 1 and 2 of antique walnut cabinet, letting dry 24 hours after wiping off excess oil.

2 Paint cabinet with cranberry; let dry.

3 Lightly sand through paint to expose the walnut color below; remove dust.

4 Apply a coat of semigloss clear wood finish, following manufacturer's directions. ✿

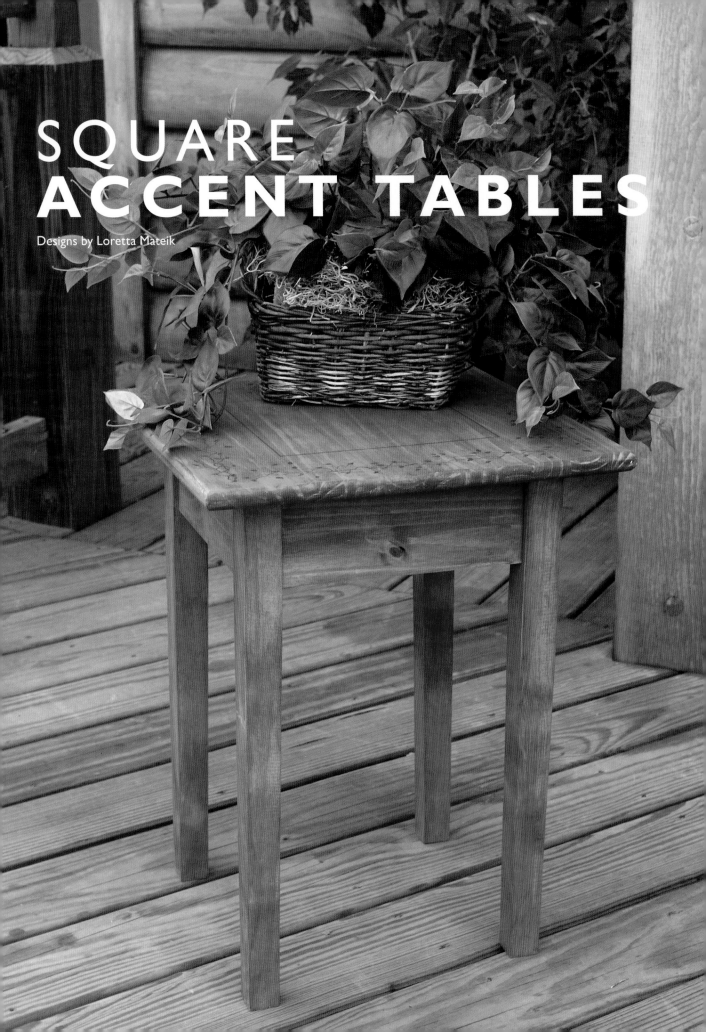

SQUARE
ACCENT TABLES

Designs by Loretta Mateik

Placed in an entryway, the family room or a corner of a kid's bedroom, these fun tables are just right for small spaces.

CUTTING

1 Use table saw to cut a 16-inch-square piece from ⅝-inch pine panel for top (B). Rout top and bottom edges with ¼-inch radius bit. **Note: Use care at corners, especially when going across the grain.**

2 From ¾x3-inch pine, cut four 9¼-inch lengths (C) for apron. Set rip fence on table saw at 2¼ inches from the center of the saw blade; set blade height at ¼ inch. On one side of each apron, cut a ⅛-inch-wide dado 2¼ inches from each end (Fig. 1).

Note: *Dadoes will be anchors for steel corner braces.*

3 From remaining 3-inch width, use band saw to cut four ¾x¾x2-inch pieces (D) for cleats.

4 From 1½-inch-square pine, cut four 19¼-inch lengths (A) for legs.

5 Using table saw and miter set at 1 degree of taper (or ¼-inch per foot), cut two adjacent sides of each leg, beginning taper 4 inches from the top (Fig. 2). Mark corners with tapered cuts

at top and bottom of leg; this will be the inside corner of the table leg when assembled.

6 Using the hand planer, shave off approximately ³⁄₁₆ inch of top 4 inches on inside corner of each leg. Measure 1⅝ inches from top of leg on planed surface and drill a ³⁄₁₆-inch hole 1½ inches deep for hanger bolt. (Fig. 3)

7 Fill any imperfections on wood surfaces with wood filler; let dry and sand smooth. Remove dust.

PROJECT SIZE
16x16x20 inches

TOOLS
• Table saw
• Router with ¼-inch radius bit
• Band saw
• Miter gauge
• Small hand planer
• Drill with ⅛-inch and ³⁄₁₆-inch bits and Phillips driver bit
• Two crescent wrenches

SUPPLIES FOR ONE TABLE
• ⅝x18-inch edge-glued pine panel: 18 inches
• ¾x3-inch pine*: 4 feet
• 1½-inch-square pine: 8 feet
• Four ¼-20 2½-inch-long hanger bolts
• Four ¼-20 wing nuts
• Two ¼-20 nuts

• Four table leg steel corner braces #27A31 from Woodcraft
• Eight #10x1-inch round-head Phillips wood screws
• Sixteen ⅝-inch Phillips wood screws
• Sandpaper
• Wood filler

Measurements given are actual, not nominal. Standard nominal lumber will need to be ripped to size.

For Trailing Ivy Table
• Americana maple #AMS11 Water-Based Stain from DecoArt
• Americana dark chocolate #DA65 acrylic paint from DecoArt
• Staining/antiquing medium from DecoArt
• Paintbrushes: 1-inch glaze/wash, #4 filbert and #1 script
• Americana matte spray sealer #DAS13
• Masking tape

For Fanciful Fun
• Masking tape
• Americana acrylic paint from DecoArt: dioxazine purple #DA101, Santa red #DA170, cadmium yellow #DA10, Hauser light green #DA131, calypso blue #DA234 and lavender #DA34
• Craft Twinkles acrylic glitter paint from DecoArt: lime green #DCT16 and galaxy blue #DCT18
• Paintbrushes: 1-inch glaze/wash, #2 round and #1 script
• 1-inch check stencil
• ⅜-inch stencil brush
• Americana Matte Spray Sealer #DAS13

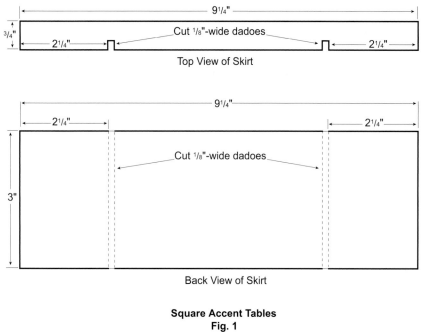

Cut 1/8"-wide dadoes

9 1/4"

3/4"

2 1/4"

2 1/4"

Top View of Skirt

9 1/4"

2 1/4"

2 1/4"

Cut 1/8"-wide dadoes

3"

Back View of Skirt

Square Accent Tables
Fig. 1

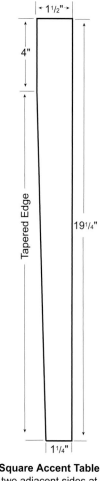

1 1/2"

4"

Tapered Edge

19 1/4"

1 1/4"

Square Accent Table Leg
Taper two adjacent sides at a 1° angle
Fig. 2

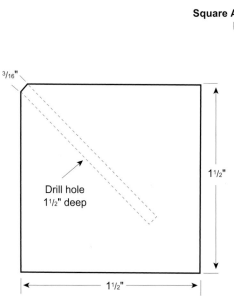

3/16"

1 1/2"

Drill hole
1 1/2" deep

1 1/2"

Square Accent Tables
Top View of Leg
Fig. 3

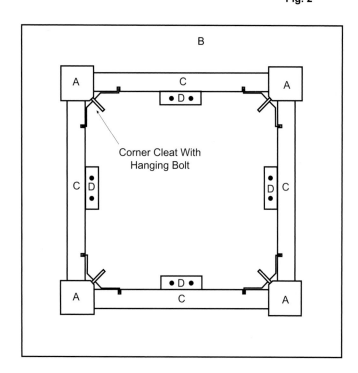

B

A

A

C

• D •

C

D

D

C

Corner Cleat With
Hanging Bolt

A

A

• D •

C

Square Accent Tables
Bottom View of Table
Fig. 4

ASSEMBLY DIAGRAM

SQUARE ACCENT TABLES CUTTING CHART (Actual Sizes)				
P	T	W	L	#
A	1½"	1½"	19¼"	4
B	⅝"	16"	16"	1
C	¾"	3"	9¼"	4
D	¾"	¾"	2"	4

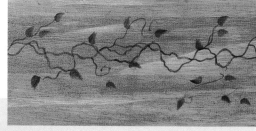

49 WATER-BASED STAIN

Safe, nontoxic and quick-drying, water-based stains can be reactivated by applying another coat for uniform coverage and clean up with soap and water. Prime table with a stain conditioner before applying the stain.

50 FREEHAND PAINTED DESIGN

A narrow script brush creates delicate vines, while a filbert brush makes it easy to paint perfect leaf shapes every time.

26 STAIN CONDITIONER

To reduce splotching and uneven staining when finishing soft woods such as pine, use a wood conditioner to seal the surface partially.

TRAILING IVY TABLE

ASSEMBLE

1 Thread both ¼-20 nuts onto the machine-thread end of hanger bolt to make a bolt head; use crescent wrenches to thread nuts in opposite directions together until tight. Using crescent wrench, thread hanger bolt into ³⁄₁₆-inch hole on table leg (A) until threads are no longer visible. Twist nuts apart to loosen and remove from bolt.

Repeat for remaining three legs.

2 Referring to assembly diagram, loosely assemble legs (A) and skirt pieces (C) using steel corner braces and wing nuts. Screw in two ⅝-inch Phillips screws per bracket, making sure legs and apron pieces are evenly spaced. Add remaining ⅝-inch screws and tighten wing nuts on hanger bolts.

3 Place top (B) face down on work surface. Lightly draw pencil lines from corner to corner to assist in assembly. Center leg/skirt assembly on underside of top, aligning corners with pencil guides. Referring to Fig. 4, glue cleats (D) to aprons and tabletop; let dry. Drill ⅛-inch pilot holes and secure with two 1-inch screws per cleat.

Finishes

TRAILING IVY TABLE

1 Remove table legs (optional). Lightly dampen table and legs with water; let dry. Sand smooth and remove dust.

2 Following manufacturer's directions, apply maple stain to all surfaces of table and legs.

3 Mix equal parts dark chocolate and staining/antiquing medium. Using vine pattern as a guide, paint vine on table with script paintbrush; let dry. *Note: Vine pattern is provided as a reference for freehand painting. It is recommended that pattern not be transferred to table for painting. If desired, enlarge 133 percent for full-size pattern. If a darker shade is desired, paint over vines a second time.*

4 Using stain mixture and filbert paintbrush, randomly apply leaves to vine; let dry. Repeat, if desired, as for vines.

5 Use masking tape to mask off an 8½-inch square in center of table. Using stain mixture and script paintbrush, paint a narrow line around inside of square; let dry. Repeat if desired.

6 Apply several light coats of matte sealer, following manufacturer's directions. Reattach legs.

FANCIFUL FUN

1 Remove table legs (optional). Sand table and legs; remove dust.

2 *Notes: Referring to Fig. 5, use masking tape to mask off each section on tabletop as it is painted.*

Apply multiple coats of paint as needed for complete coverage, allowing to dry after each application. Base-coat 5-inch corner squares with dioxazine purple; remove masking tape. Base-coat table legs with calypso blue.

3 Divide each rectangle between corner squares into three 2-inch sections. Paint outer 2-inch sections of each rectangle with glitter paint,

FANCIFUL FUN

6 ACRYLIC PAINT

Water-based and nontoxic, DecoArt's Americana acrylic paint is an all-purpose paint for decorative painting, home decor and general craft painting for use on almost any surface.

51 ADD PIZZAZ

Add sparkle to your projects without the mess of sprinkle-on glitter. DecoArt Craft Twinkle paint contains large flakes of glitter suspended in an acrylic base.

following manufacturer's directions; re-move masking tape. Base-coat middle sections with cadmium yellow, then apply checkerboard pattern using check stencil and Santa red; remove masking tape.

4 Referring to Fig. 5, paint flowers freehand on two opposite corner squares, using cadmium yellow for petals and Hauser light green for stems and leaves; add a dot of Santa red in centers of petals. Paint random spirals on remaining corner squares using cadmium yellow.

5 Flip tabletop over, supporting it in the center, unpainted square area. Base-coat sides of table with lime green; base-coat underside edges of tabletop with dioxazine purple.

6 Flip tabletop back over; base-coat center square with lavender; remove masking tape.

7 Apply several light coats of matte sealer, following manufacturer's directions. Reattach legs. ❀

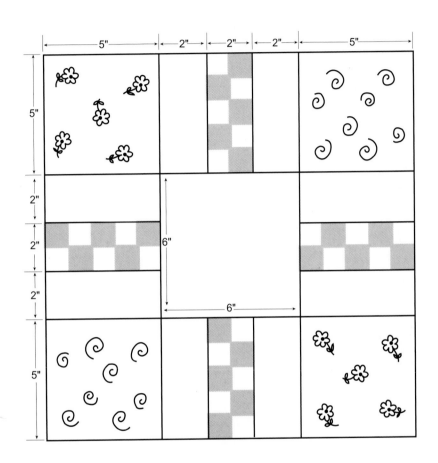

Square Accent Tables
Fig. 5

Square Accent Tables
Vine
Enlarge 133%

FAUX ANTIQUE
BENCHES

Designs by June Fiechter

Turn a simple bench into a timeless treasure for an elegant dressing area, or give your little cowpokes a special place to sit and pull on their boots.

CUTTING

1 Cut ¾-inch plywood to 30x34 inches for bench back. Enlarge pattern for top edge 200 percent and transfer to top of bench back, flipping pattern at center to do both sides; cut out using scroll saw.

2 Cut ¾x11-inch pine into two 16-inch lengths for bench sides.

3 Cut 1x4 pine into two 23¼-inch lengths for front and back supports.

4 Cut ¾x12-inch pine to a 28-inch length for bench top.

5 Sand surfaces and cut edges of wood with medium-grit sandpaper.

ASSEMBLE

Note: Countersink all holes for screws when drilling.

1 Place bench back on flat work surface. Position sides on back 2 inches from each edge with bottom

---

PROJECT SIZE
30x34x11 inches

TOOLS
• Band saw
• Scroll saw
• Drill

SUPPLIES FOR ONE BENCH
• ¾-inch Baltic birch plywood*: 30x34-inch piece
• ¾x11-inch pine*: 4 feet
• 1x4 pine: 6 feet
• ¾x12-inch pine*: 3 feet
• Medium- and fine-grit sandpaper
• Wood glue
• 1¼-inch wood screws
• Wood putty
• Masking tape
• Soft cloth

Measurements given are actual, not nominal. Standard nominal lumber will need to be ripped to size.

For Western Star Bench
• Stiff-bristled paintbrush

• Americana acrylic paint from DecoArt: French vanilla #DA184, light parchment #DA243, antique white #DA58, buttermilk #DA03, light buttermilk #DA164, sand #DA04 and light cinnamon #DA114
• Americana Stuccos from DecoArt: natural #AST02 and light ecru #AST04
• Aluminum foil
• Natural Tin-Tiques stars from DC&C: two 3-inch #24-8005 and one 4-inch #24-8007
• Heavenly Hues plaster and ceramic wash from DecoArt: earth brown #DHH06 and soft black #DHH02
• Plastercraft Spray matte finish #DAS13 from DecoArt
• Four silver upholstery tacks

For Floral Fabric Bench
• Royal Coat Decoupage Finish #1401 from Plaid

• Paper napkin, wrapping paper, wallpaper or decorative scrapbook paper with repeating pattern
• Flat paintbrushes
• Gallery Glass Window Color from Plaid: orange poppy #16005, magenta royal #16017, ruby red #16015, berry red #16023, amethyst #16014, emerald green #16009, royal blue #16012, kelly green #16008, ivy green #16024, slate blue #16013, lime green #16035 and blue diamond #16011
• Gallery Glass Mediums: matte #16048 and crackle #16047
• FolkArt Antiquing Medium from Plaid: down home brown #811 and woodn' bucket brown #817
• 1-inch foam brushes
• FolkArt acrylic paint from Plaid: peach #949
• FolkArt matte #864 Outdoor Sealer from Plaid

52 PLASTER AND CERAMIC WASH

Heavenly Hues paint can be applied directly to stucco or ceramic finish with no pretreatment. Create an antique wash or pickled look simply by brushing on and wiping off.

53 PURCHASED ADD-ONS

Push purchased tin shapes into the wet stucco medium on the bench's back to make a sparkling impression. This is an easy way to change the look of a project.

54 FAUX LEATHER WITH FOIL

Crumpled aluminum foil is carefully pressed into a thin layer of wet stucco medium on the seat of this bench to create a faux leather seat.

WESTERN STYLE BENCH

55 MATTE SPRAY SEALER

Plastercraft Spray acrylic sealer is a low-odor, nonyellowing, weatherproof coating that dries fast and provides permanent protection.

edges flush. Position back support on bench back between sides with top edge of support flush with top edges of sides. Mark all positions with pencil.

2 Glue back support to sides; let dry. Secure with two screws through each side. Reposition on bench back and glue in place; let dry. Secure back support to back with three screws.

3 Glue front support to front edges of sides with top edges flush; let dry. Secure with two screws through each side.

4 Glue top in place; let dry.

5 Fill all holes with wood putty; let dry and sand smooth. Remove dust.

Finishes

WESTERN STAR BENCH

1 Using a stiff-bristled paintbrush and all paint colors *except cinnamon*, paint bench top, sides and front support with short, choppy strokes, applying each color randomly and being careful not to blend colors.

2 Mask off center of bench top 1½ inches from edges. Apply a heavy coat of both natural and light ecru Stuccos inside masked area. Crumple a piece of aluminum foil and unwrap, then press into wet Stuccos and remove to create texture.

3 Apply Stuccos to bench back in same manner as for bench top, applying more heavily in upper center and tapering off toward outer edges. Press 4-inch tin star into Stuccos in center of bench back; position 3-inch tin stars on each side of center star and press into Stuccos to secure.

4 Let all stucco areas dry completely, then sand well with medium-grit sandpaper and remove dust.

5 Using a soft cloth, apply a light coat of cinnamon to stucco area of seat, rubbing excess paint off of raised areas. Let dry, then rub hard with soft cloth. Repeat process with earth brown, then soft black.

6 Paint bench back in same manner as remainder of bench in step 1, leaving stars unpainted; let dry.

7 Spray bench with several light coats of matte finish following manufacturer's directions. Hammer silver upholstery tacks into corners of the faux leather on bench top.

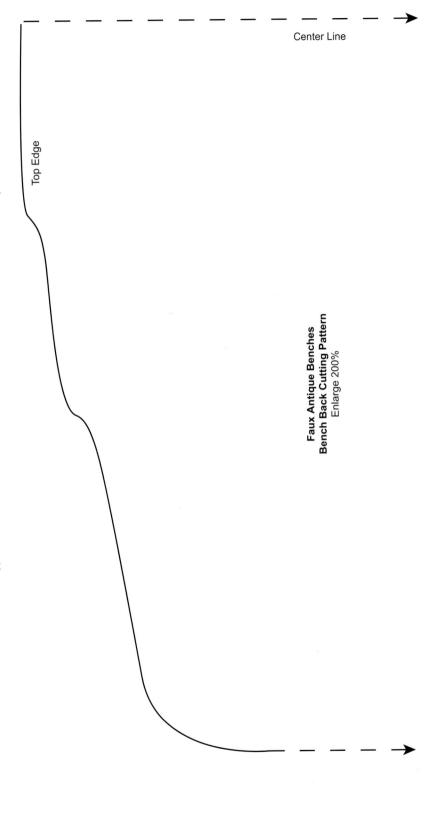

Center Line

Top Edge

Faux Antique Benches
Bench Back Cutting Pattern
Enlarge 200%

57 TRANSPARENT COLOR

Gallery Glass Window Color by Plaid, applied over the decoupaged paper on the bench's back, dries clearly enough to reveal the paper's pattern, but will leave a hint of color and texture.

56 FAUX FABRIC DECOUPAGE

Use Plaid's Royal Coat decoupage finish with elegant rolled wrapping paper or wallpaper to create this bench's faux fabric back. Royal Coat decoupage is acid free and dries quickly to a hard, satin finish.

59 AGED LEATHER

Apply a heavy layer of Gallery Glass Crackle Medium over the painted seat area. This will turn clear as it dries, leaving large cracks reminiscent of aged leather.

58 OUTDOOR SEALER

This polyurethane-based, brush-on finish gives maximum durability for outdoor projects. It seals and protects against harsh outdoor conditions.

FLORAL FABRIC BENCH

60 ANTIQUING OVER CRACKLE MEDIUM

Rub in a small amount of this antiquing medium over the entire bench with a soft cloth to imitate the old, gently used look of antique furniture.

FLORAL FABRIC BENCH

1 Following manufacturer's directions, apply paper to back of bench using decoupage medium, then carefully brush medium over top of paper. Let dry completely.

2 Using flat paintbrush, paint desired window color over decoupaged paper, leaving ridges for texture. Let dry.

3 Mask off center of bench top 2 inches from edges. Randomly apply a heavy coat each of orange poppy, magenta royale, ruby red and berry red inside masked area. Let dry.

4 Using a circular motion, apply a heavy coat of crackle medium directly from bottle to painted area of bench seat. Let dry. **Note:** *There should be a thick, white layer covering painted area, but use care not to overlap tape.* Crackling medium will become clear as it dries, and create large cracks.

5 Use soft cloth to rub woodn' bucket brown antiquing medium generously over dried crackle finish, then immediately wipe off, leaving medium only in crevices. Let dry, then apply several coats of matte medium over crackled area.

6 Remove masking tape carefully. Using foam brush, paint remaining areas of bench with peach. **Note:** *Use flat brush to get close to crackled area. Let dry overnight.*

7 Use soft cloth to rub small amounts of down home brown antiquing medium over entire bench. Let dry.

8 Apply several light coats of matte finish to entire bench, following manufacturer's directions. ✿

PEDESTAL PLANT STANDS

Designs by June Fiechter

Faux finishes take center stage with these two plant stands. Simple construction allows you to focus on the finish, resulting in a project that's simply sensational!

CUTTING

1 Cut 1x4 into four 19-inch lengths for sides.

2 From ¾-inch birch plywood, cut two 7-inch-square pieces for supports, and two 10-inch-square pieces for top and bottom.

ASSEMBLE

1 Glue four 19-inch side pieces together to make a 4¼x4¼x19-inch pedestal (Fig. 1). Let dry.

2 Glue 7-inch-square supports, centered, to ends of pedestal. Let dry.

3 Glue 10-inch-square top and bottom, centered, to supports.

PROJECT SIZE
10x10x21¾ inches

TOOLS
• Soft cloth
• Table saw or band saw

SUPPLIES FOR ONE PLANT STAND
• 1x4 pine: 8 feet
• ¾ -inch birch plywood: 2x2-foot piece
• Wood glue
• Medium and fine-grit sandpaper
• Foam brushes

For Copper & Steel Plant Stand
• Sophisticated Finishes Primer and Clear Sealer from Triangle Coatings Inc.
• Sophisticated Finishes Metallic Surfacer from Triangle Coatings Inc.: copper and silver blue
• Sophisticated Finishes patina green Antiquing Solution from Triangle Coatings Inc.
• Sophisticated Finishes black Tinting Solution from Triangle Coatings Inc.

For Marble Plant Stand
• Ceramcoat All-Purpose Sealer from Delta
• Ceramcoat acrylic paint from Delta: white #2505, mudstone #2488, putty #2460, eggshell white #2539 and barn red #2490
• Renaissance Foil Adhesive from Delta
• Gold Renaissance Foil from Delta
• Steel wool
• Soft cloth
• Ceramcoat Faux Finish Glaze Base from Delta
• Sea sponge

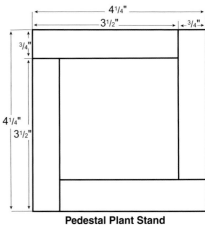

Pedestal Plant Stand
Fig. 1
Top View of Pedestal

61 ANTIQUING FOR AGED METAL

Apply the antiquing solution by Triangle Coatings while the final coat of metallic surfacer is still slightly tacky. Drying time varies greatly, depending on temperature, humidity and air circulation. The patina will begin to develop in a few minutes.

62 METALLIC SURFACERS

Sophisticated Finishes Metallic Surfacers by Triangle Coatings are a blend of finely ground metal particles in an acrylic sealing compound. Most applications will require at least two coats. This finish cleans up with water.

COPPER & STEEL PLANT STAND

MARBLE PLANT STAND

63 FAUX MARBLE

Delta Faux Finish Glaze Base, mixed with acrylic paint, dries slowly and gives you more time to work. Create the elegant veining found in real marble with a foam brush and several paint colors.

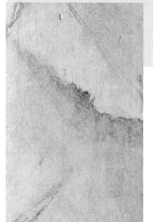

64 GOLD LEAFING

Delta Renaissance foil is economical, versatile and easy to use. It's nontoxic and water-based, so even kids can apply the beautiful, high-quality look of actual gold leafing.

4 Sand well with medium- then fine-grit sandpaper; remove dust.

Finishes

COPPER & STEEL PLANT STAND

1 Seal wood surfaces with primer and clear sealer; let dry.

2 Paint top, bottom and supports with two heavy coats of copper metallic surfacer, using a daubing motion with the side of the sponge brush. Let dry completely.

3 Lightly dab copper metallic surfacer over same areas; before it dries completely, apply a coat of patina green antiquing solution. Let set.

4 Paint pedestal with two coats of silver blue metallic surfacer; let dry completely.

5 Paint black Tinting Solution in vertical strokes over blue metallic surfacer; let set 3 or 4 minutes. *Note: Solution will separate as it sets.*

6 Use paper towels to wipe pedestal with a vertical motion. Let dry.

MARBLE PLANT STAND

1 Apply a coat of sealer over all surfaces of stand; let dry.

2 Paint top and bottom of stand with barn red; let dry. Brush a coat of foil adhesive over paint and let dry 20 minutes, then apply a second coat of adhesive; let dry. Press foil onto adhesive using a foam brush. Lightly rub over foil surfaces with steel wool to age. Wipe clean with soft cloth. Apply

sealer over foiled areas.

3 Paint pedestal and supports with eggshell white; let dry.

4 Mix mudstone with glaze base. Create marbled effect on pedestal and supports by dipping the broad, flat side of a foam brush into a small amount of paint mixture, pushing brush on surface to create random, jagged lines, then pulling brush back from line, feathering and softening edges. Repeat process with putty.

5 Dip chisel end of foam brush into mudstone paint mixture and create random vein lines on pedestal and supports; let dry.

6 Mix eggshell white with glaze base and paint over marbled area with foam brush.

7 Dip damp sea sponge in white paint and lightly dab over marbling. Let dry. ❋

ASIAN INSPIRED SCONCES

Designs by Myra Risley Perrin

Make your rooms sparkle with these decorative and functional projects. Pair them on a wall or sit one on the edge of a shelf for some interesting illumination.

PROJECT SIZE
6x15x6 inches

TOOLS
- Band saw, scroll saw or jigsaw
- Drill press or hand-held drill with ⁵⁄₁₆ - and 1⅛ -inch drill or forstner bits
- Biscuit jointer
- Clamps
- Straight edge
- Nail set
- U-shaped gouge

SUPPLIES FOR ONE SCONCE
- ¾x4⅝ -inch walnut*: 3 feet
- ½x½ -inch walnut*: 6 feet
- ½x½ -inch maple*: 4 feet
- Four #3 biscuits
- Wood glue
- Sandpaper
- Double-sided carpet tape
- 4¾ x12⁷⁄₁₆ piece of rice paper or other decorative paper

- Spray bottle of water
- Heavy objects for weighting
- 1-inch finish nails
- Hanging hardware
- Electric candle lamp

Measurements given are actual, not nominal. Standard nominal lumber will need to be ripped to size.

For Walnut & Maple Sconce
- Deft semigloss lacquer
- Renaissance Wax polish

For Modern Metallic Sconce
- Black acrylic paint Golden graphite gray #9250615 heavy-bodied artist acrylic
- Silver Rub 'n Buff wax-based metallic finish

For Good Luck Sconce
- Cream-color acrylic paint
- Crackle medium
- Golden Quinacridone burnt orange #9252103 fluid artist acrylic

CUTTING

1 From ¾x4⅝-inch walnut, cut two 4⅜-inch lengths for top and bottom, and one 12½-inch length for back.

2 From ½x½-inch walnut, cut four 15-inch lengths. From ½x½-inch maple, cut seven 6-inch lengths. Sand smooth and remove dust.

3 Using 1⅛-inch bit, drill a hole centered on back, 1 inch from bottom edge. Use U-shaped gouge to carve a vertical groove below hole to accommodate electric cord.

4 Using ⁵⁄₁₆-inch bit, drill six holes evenly spaced in top (Fig. 1).

5 Cut two biscuit joints in face of back, at top and bottom edges; cut corresponding biscuit joints on back edges of top and bottom pieces. Dry-fit top and bottom to back with biscuits, then glue and clamp until dry. Sand smooth and remove dust.

WALNUT & MAPLE SCONCE

4 SEMIGLOSS LACQUER

This Deft product can be applied with a brush or sprayed on for a baby-safe, fast-drying, crystal-clear finish on furniture, cabinets, paneling, antiques and crafts.

65 WAX FINISH

A rubbed-wax finish protects against the damaging effects of humidity, heat, dust, aging and ordinary wear with a durable, lustrous protective coating. Renaissance Wax was developed by the British Museum to safeguard its precious items.

MODERN METALLIC SCONCE

66 HEAVY BODY ACRYLICS

This acrylic paint by Golden is formulated with pure pigments in a 100-percent acrylic emulsion, offering excellent permanency and lightfastness. Heavy body colors contain no additives such as matting agents, so the gloss of each color will be different.

67 WAX-BASED METALLIC FINISH

Rub 'n Buff, a product made from imported carnauba waxes, metallic powders and pigments, is rubbed onto any surface with a soft cloth, then buffed to a lustrous finish.

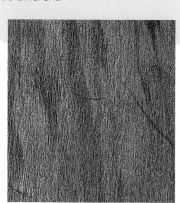

ASSEMBLE

1 Clamp straight edge to work surface, forming a right angle with edge of surface. Place strips of double-sided carpet tape on work surface below straight edge. Referring to Fig. 2, position four 15-inch lengths of ½-inch-square walnut parallel to the surface edge, with ends even with straight edge.

2 Position the top and bottom 6-inch lengths of ½-inch maple horizontally across 15-inch strips, spacing as shown; position the three center 6-inch strips as shown.

3 Glue strips in place to make screen; let dry. **Note:** *Remaining two strips will be glued in place after screen is attached.*

Finishes

WALNUT & MAPLE SCONCE

1 Spray assembled pieces with lacquer, following manufacturer's directions, then apply wax polish. **Note:** *Do not finish back of screen or front edges of top and bottom; paper will be glued to these surfaces.*

2 Cut a 4¾x12⁷⁄₁₆-inch piece of rice paper. Thin wood glue with

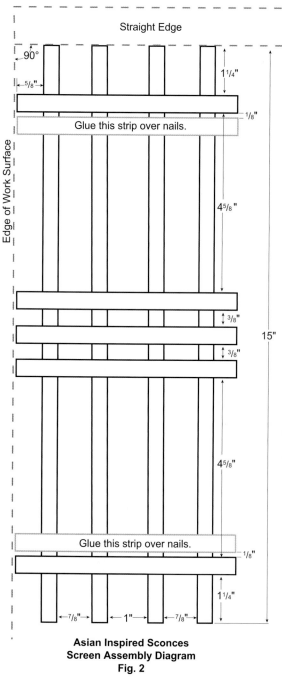

Straight Edge

90°

⁵/₈"

1¹/₄"

¹/₈"

Glue this strip over nails.

Edge of Work Surface

4⁵/₈"

3/8"

3/8"

15"

4⁵/₈"

Glue this strip over nails.

¹/₈"

1¹/₄"

⁷/₈"   1"   ⁷/₈"

**Asian Inspired Sconces
Screen Assembly Diagram
Fig. 2**

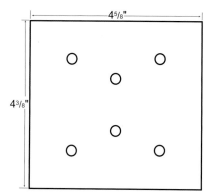

4⁵/₈"

4³/₈"

**Asian Inspired Sconces
Top View of Sconce Top**
Drill six ⁵/₁₆" holes evenly spaced
Fig. 1

68 ARTISTS' ACRYLIC
This paint gives intense, permanent acrylic colors produced from lightfast pigments, not dyes, and offers strong colors with thin consistencies.

68

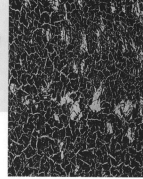

GOOD LUCK
SCONCE

water and spread over back of screen, then carefully place paper over glued area, smoothing out any wrinkles. Let dry. Lightly mist both sides of paper with water; place screen paper side down on work surface and weight corners with heavy objects to keep flat. Let paper dry.

3 Remove weights and adhere a strip of double-sided tape across top and bottom edges of paper on screen; press screen in place on fronts of top and bottom pieces. Using finish nails, secure screen to front edges through vertical strips; set nails. Glue remaining 6-inch maple strips in place over nail holes.

4 Attach hanging hardware to back following manufacturer's directions. Place electric candle lamp inside sconce and pull cord through hole in back.

MODERN METALLIC SCONCE

1 Paint assembled pieces black. Following manufacturer's directions, apply silver Rub 'n Buff over black paint. **Note:** *Do not finish back of screen or front edges of top and bottom; paper will be glued to these surfaces.*

2 Finish sconce following steps 2–4 of the Walnut & Maple Sconce.

GOOD LUCK SCONCE

1 Use cream-color acrylic paint for base coat. Following manufacturer's directions, apply crackle medium and Quinacridone burnt orange for the top coat. **Note:** *Do not finish back of screen or front edges of top and bottom; paper will be glued to these surfaces.*

2 Finish sconce following steps 2–4 of the Walnut & Maple Sconce. ✽

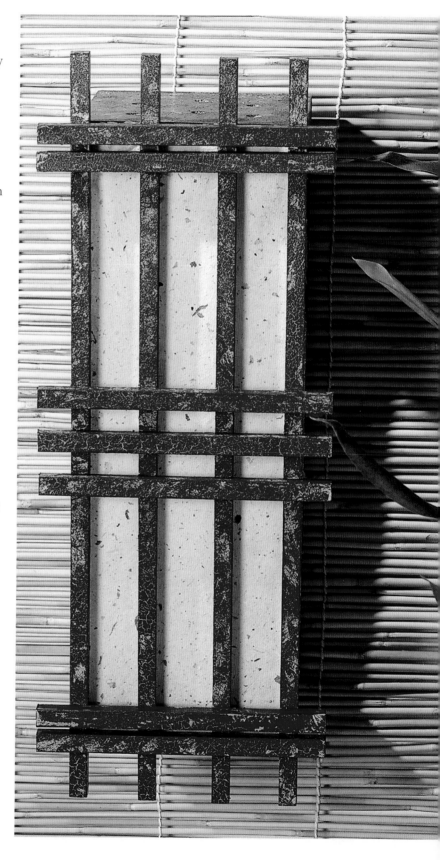

TEA
TRAYS

Designs by Loretta Mateik

As easy to build as they are elegant, these two serving pieces will let you treat your guests like royalty with breakfast in bed, iced tea on the front porch or a picnic under the ancient oak in the backyard.

CUTTING

1 From ½-inch poplar plywood, use band saw to cut two 2¼x13½-inch pieces for tray sides, and two 3¼x11-inch pieces for tray ends.

2 Enlarge pattern for tray end handle 125 percent. Copy pattern for tray side decorative edge on plain paper, placing on fold as indicated to make full-size pattern; cut out. Use graphite paper to transfer patterns to appropriate wood pieces; cut out with scroll saw.

3 Use band saw to cut one 11x14½-inch piece from ⅛-inch birch plywood for tray bottom.

4 Sand pieces smooth and remove dust.

ASSEMBLE

1 Glue and nail tray ends to tray sides; glue and nail tray bottom in place. Let dry.

2 Set nails and fill holes with wood putty. Sand smooth and remove dust.

Finishes

DECOUPAGED TEA TRAY

1 Cut design from napkin and separate plies. Center napkin on tray bottom and very lightly outline with white chalk pencil; remove napkin. Apply decoupage medium to outlined area, then carefully apply napkin design, smoothing out wrinkles. Thin decoupage medium with water and apply several coats over napkin, letting dry at least 15 minutes after each coat.

2 Add a few drops of trail tan to a small amount of old parchment; base-coat remainder of tray bottom with mixture. Let dry.

3 Using photo as a guide, randomly paint block patterns using additional colors. **Note:** *Soften colors slightly with white, if desired.* Let dry.

4 Apply several light coats of clear sealer following manufacturer's directions.

PROJECT SIZE
14½x11x3⅜ inches

TOOLS
- Band saw
- Scroll saw
- Nail set

For Still Life Tea Tray
- Woodburner with cone point

SUPPLIES FOR ONE TEA TRAY
- 24x24-inch piece ½-inch poplar plywood
- 12x16-inch piece ⅛-inch Baltic birch plywood
- Graphite paper
- Sandpaper
- Wood glue
- 1-inch brads
- Wood putty
- Paintbrushes

For Decoupaged Tea Tray
- Decorative paper napkin
- White chalk pencil
- Mod-Podge decoupage medium
- Ceramcoat acrylic paint from Delta: old parchment #2092, trail tan #2435, white #2505 and three additional colors to match napkin for block background
- Make It Last! Clear Coat Sealer from Krylon

For Still Life Tea Tray
- Ceramcoat acrylic paint from Delta: leaf green #2067, brown iron oxide #2023, golden brown #2054, Moroccan red #2552 and vintage wine #2434
- Soft cloth (optional)
- Cotton swabs
- Fruitwood gel stain
- Matte varnish

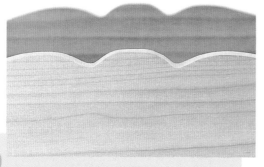

69

69 SPRAY-ON SEALANT

This spray-on product protects and seals any painted surface including wood, glass, metal, paper and plastic.

6 ACRYLIC PAINT

Water-based acrylic paint is made up of tiny particles of plastic acrylic resin and pigment suspended in water. As the water evaporates, the resin particles fuse together, forming a strong, durable paint. It cleans up easily with soap and water when wet, and is permanent when dry.

6

70

DECOUPAGED
TEA TRAY

70 PAPER NAPKIN DECOUPAGE

Nontoxic and water-based, Mod-Podge by Plaid dries quickly and can be sanded to a smooth finish. It dries clear and cleans up easily while wet with soap and water.

STILL LIFE TEA TRAY

1 Enlarge fruit pattern 117 percent. Use graphite paper to transfer enlarged pattern to center bottom of tray. Draw a straight line ½ inch from each edge for border, as shown.

2 Use woodburner to trace transferred lines. Thin paint with water to the consistency of ink and paint fruit as follows:

Apple—*leaf green.*
Pear—*golden brown*; shade with *Moroccan red.*
Grapes—*vintage wine.*
Stems—*brown iron oxide.*

3 Using either a brush or a soft cloth, stain the remainder of the tray with fruitwood gel stain according to manufacturer's directions. ***Note:*** *Use cotton swabs to immediately wipe off* *any stain that may get on fruit design. Let dry.*

4 Apply three or four light coats of matte varnish, following manufacturer's directions. ❀

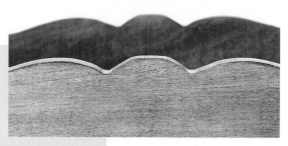

71 WOOD STAIN GEL

This product from Delta has a thick, creamy formula for no drips or runs. Brush it on and wipe it off like traditional stains. Nontoxic and water-based, this stain gel is easy to clean, dries fast and has little odor.

STILL LIFE TEA TRAY

72 WOODBURNING

Use an electric woodburning tool to create lines and shading on wood surfaces. Don't overdo it— step back periodically to check your work.

Tea Trays
Tray Side Decorative Edge
Cut on fold from paper to make
full-size pattern

Place on fold

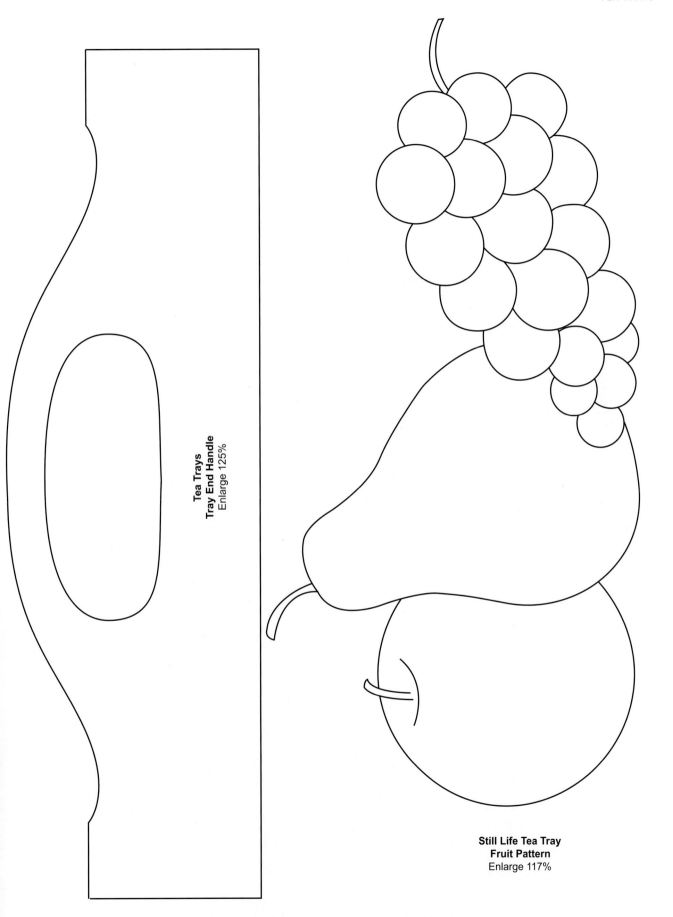

Tea Trays
Tray End Handle
Enlarge 125%

Still Life Tea Tray
Fruit Pattern
Enlarge 117%

JEWELRY CADDY
DUET

Designs by Patti J. Ryan

Bring order to your dressing table and keep your favorite accessories within easy reach with these unique swivel jewelry cases.

CUTTING

1 From ³⁄₈-inch plywood, cut one 8-inch-diameter circle (for swivel base top) and one 6-inch-diameter circle (for swivel base bottom).

2 Use table saw to cut a ¹⁄₈-inch-wide by ¹⁄₁₆-inch-deep groove centered down the length of one 24-inch length of ¹⁄₄x2¹⁄₂-inch pine; cut two 10-inch lengths (for sides) from grooved length. From remaining 24-inch length, cut two 7-inch lengths (for top and bottom).

3 From ¹⁄₄-inch birch plywood, cut one 6⁵⁄₈x10-inch piece (for dividing board), and one 3x7³⁄₄-inch piece (for top cap).

4 From screen molding, cut four 6³⁄₈-inch lengths (for hook supports).

5 Sand cut edges smooth; remove dust.

ASSEMBLE

1 Following manufacturer's directions, attach 4-inch turntable mechanism to swivel base top and swivel base bottom. Fill screw holes and any gaps on cut edges of plywood circles with wood filler; let dry and sand smooth, rounding top edge of swivel base top slightly. Set aside.

2 Referring to Fig. 1, mark placement of hook supports on front and on back of dividing board; glue and clamp supports in place. Let dry. Mark position of hooks on supports and drill pilot holes.

PROJECT SIZE
Case: 8³⁄₈x10⁵⁄₈x3³⁄₈ inches, excluding knob
Swivel Base: 8x1¹⁄₄ inches

TOOLS
• Table saw
• Saber saw
• Miter saw
• Drill
• Clamps
• Nail set

SUPPLIES FOR ONE CADDY
• 10x15-inch scrap of ³⁄₈-inch paint-grade plywood
• ¹⁄₄x2¹⁄₂-inch pine or poplar*: two 24-inch lengths
• 12x12-inch scrap of ¹⁄₄-inch birch plywood
• ¹⁄₈x⁵⁄₈-inch screen molding: 3 feet
• ⁵⁄₈-inch-wide decorative molding: 2 feet
• ³⁄₈-inch-wide decorative molding: 2 feet
• 150- and 220-grit sandpaper
• 4-inch turntable mechanism
• Wood filler
• Crafter's Pick Sand-N-Stain wood glue from API
• Brads
• Porcelain or brass drawer knob with screw
• Sixteen 1¹⁄₄-inch curtain-rod hooks, or cup hooks
• Americana Stain Conditioner from DecoArt
• Americana mahogany #AMS09 Water-Based Stain from DecoArt
• Americana Satins satin varnish #DSA28 from DecoArt
• Paste wax

Measurements given are actual, not nominal. Standard nominal lumber will need to be ripped to size.

For Mahogany Caddy
• Americana shimmering silver #DA70 Dazzling Metallics from DecoArt
• Nickel-finish upholstery tacks
• Krylon Silver Leafing Pen #9902

For Suede Caddy
• Americana glorious gold #DA71 Dazzling Metallics from DecoArt
• Brass-finish upholstery tacks
• Masking tape
• Krylon Berber #1240 Make It Suede! texture paint
• Krylon Gold Leafing Pen #9901

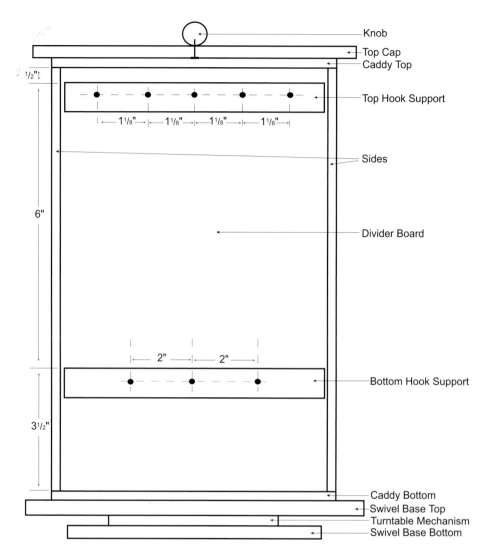

**Jewelry Caddy Duet
Fig. 1**

3 Slip dividing board into grooves on sides; position top and bottom and attach to sides with brads.

4 Drill a hole for knob screw in center of top cap; countersink for screw head. Insert screw in hole. Center top cap on top of caddy; glue and attach with brads.

5 Cut ⅝-inch-wide decorative molding, mitering edges to fit

around top cap flush with top edge; glue and attach with brads. Repeat with ⅜-inch-wide decorative molding, cutting to fit around bottom of caddy.

Finishes
MAHOGANY CADDY

1 Sand all surfaces with 150- then 220-grit sandpaper; remove dust.

2 Paint swivel base with shimmering silver; let dry, then lightly wet sand

and wipe clean. Apply a second coat; let dry. Press nickel-finish upholstery tacks evenly around edge of swivel base top.

3 Following manufacturer's directions, apply stain conditioner to caddy. Apply mahogany stain following manufacturer's directions, lightly sanding between coats with 220-grit sandpaper.

4 Apply satin varnish to stained surfaces, following manufacturer's directions.

5 Add detail to decorative molding with silver leafing pen; let dry.

6 Screw hooks into supports. Attach knob to top of caddy.

7 Apply a coat of paste wax to stained surfaces; let dry five minutes, then buff to a soft sheen.

SUEDE CADDY

1 Sand all surfaces with 150- then 220-grit sandpaper; remove dust.

2 Paint swivel base with glorious gold; let dry, then lightly wet sand and wipe clean. Apply a second coat; let dry. Press brass-finish upholstery btacks evenly around edge of swivel base top.

3 Following manufacturer's directions, apply stain conditioner to outside surfaces of caddy. Apply mahogany stain following manufacturer's directions, lightly sanding between coats with 220-grit sandpaper.

4 Mask outside of caddy with masking tape. Following manufacturer's directions, apply several coats of Make It Suede! texture paint to inside of caddy.

5 Apply satin varnish to stained surfaces, following manufacturer's directions.

6 Add detail to decorative molding with gold leafing pen; let dry.

7 Screw hooks into supports. Attach knob to top of caddy.

8 Apply a coat of paste wax to stained surfaces; let dry five minutes, then buff to a soft sheen. ✹

49 WATER-BASED STAIN

Safe, non-toxic and quick-drying, water-based stains can be reactivated by applying another coat for uniform coverage, and clean up with soap and water. Prime surface with a stain conditioner before applying the stain.

MAHOGANY CADDY

73 SUEDE TEXTURE

Create the luxurious look of real suede lining with this easy-to-apply spray from Krylon.

SUEDE CADDY

53 PURCHASED ADD-ONS

Upholstery tacks around the perimeter of the swivel caddy add flair to this small project.

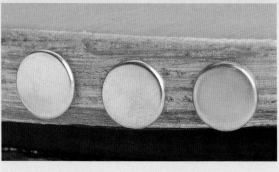

UNIQUE
ENTRY
TABLES

Design by June Fiechter

Just the right size for the front foyer or back entry, this small table makes a big impact with two fantastic finishes.

CUTTING

1 Cut ¾x11-inch pine board to 23½-inch length (A) for top.

2 Cut 1x4 into two 8-inch lengths (B) for end boards and two 22-inch lengths (C) for side boards.

3 Cut 1½x1½-inch pine into four 24-inch lengths (D) for legs.

4 Cut ⅜x1⅜-inch furring strips into two 5⅛-inch lengths (E) for end supports and two 17½-inch lengths (F) for side supports.

5 Sand edges smooth.

ASSEMBLE

1 Draw a pencil line 1½ inches from each edge on underside of top (A). Position end and side boards (B, C) on outer edge of pencil lines. Adjust fit by sanding, if needed, and remove dust; glue and nail end and side boards together to form a frame. Let dry, then apply glue to top edges of frame and glue in place on underside of top. Let dry.

2 Position legs (D) inside frame at corners and glue to secure. Glue supports (E, F) against frame between legs. *Note: Supports should fit snuggly between legs.*

3 Drill two holes through bottom of each support into, but not through, top; secure with screws.

4 Using same bit, drill and countersink holes at corners of frame into legs; secure frame to legs with screws.

5 Fill screw holes with wood putty; let dry. Sand entire piece well and remove dust.

PROJECT SIZE
23½x24¾x11 inches

TOOLS
- Band saw
- Drill

SUPPLIES FOR ONE TABLE
- ¾x11-inch pine board*: 3 feet
- 1x4 pine: 6 feet
- 1½x1½-inch pine*: 10 feet
- ⅜x1⅜-inch furring strips*: 4 feet
- Fine- and medium-grit sandpaper
- Wood glue
- Twelve ¾-inch finish nails
- Twenty ⅛ x 1¼-inch wood screws
- Wood putty
- Foam brushes, including ½ inch wide
- ¼-inch-wide painter's tape
- Paintbrushes, including 2 inch wide

Measurements given are actual, not nominal. Standard nominal lumber will need to be ripped to size.

For Faux Stone Table
- Americana acrylic paint from DecoArt: mink tan #DA92, milk chocolate #DA174, antique white #DA58, titanium white #DA01 and neutral grey #DA95
- Faux Glazing Medium #DS18 from DecoArt
- Sea sponge
- Americana Stuccos from DecoArt: natural #AST02 and light ecru #AST04
- Putty knife
- Americana Water-Based Stains from DecoArt: chestnut #AMS03
- Paper towels
- Americana Satins satin varnish from DecoArt

For Faux Mosaic Table
- Americana acrylic paint from DecoArt: citron green #DA235, baby blue #DA42, desert turquoise #DA44, colonial green #DA81, soft sage #DA207, blue violet #DA141, Hauser light green #DA131, camel #DA191, dark pine #DA49, Wedgewood blue #DA38, avocado #DA52, heritage brick #DA219 and soft black #DA155
- Weathered Wood Crackling Medium from DecoArt
- Tack cloth
- Triple Thick Gloss Glaze from DecoArt

74 FAUX STAINED GLASS

Use painter's tape to create a mosaic pattern on the table top. Apply jewel toned acrylic paint with a sponge to avoid leaving brush marks.

25 TRIPLE THICK GLAZE

This spray finish by DecoArt creates a thick, clear acrylic coating to give a glass-like illusion of depth. It goes on smoothly, dries quickly, will not yellow and is non-toxic.

FAUX MOSAIC TABLE

31 CRACKLE PAINT

A crackle medium dries clear and can be antiqued for an aged look. Apply light, even coats for tiny cracks, or two to three heavy coats for large cracks.

Finishes

FAUX MOSAIC TABLE

1 Using foam brush, paint all of table except top with avocado; paint top of table soft black. Let dry.

2 Place table on its side. Following manufacturer's directions, use foam brush to apply a heavy coat of crackling medium to side of table; allow to set, but not dry, then apply one coat of soft sage over crackle medium. *Note: Either foam brush or paintbrush can be used to apply paint over crackle medium.*

Practice first on scrap wood for desired effect. Repeat process on opposite side and both ends of table.

3 In same manner, working over same areas, apply another heavy coat of crackle medium, followed by a coat of heritage brick. While heritage brick is still wet, use edge of 2-inch paintbrush to push away the paint in random areas to create a worn appearance. Let dry. Sand lightly to smooth, then wipe with tack cloth to remove dust.

4 On tabletop, use ¼-inch-wide painter's tape to mask off tile areas. Using foam brush, paint tile areas using random colors, dabbing on a heavy amount of paint to each tile and smoothing paint as flat as possible. Let dry.

5 Spray table top with several coats of triple thick gloss glaze following manufacturer's directions. Let dry completely. Remove tape.

FAUX STONE TABLE

1 Draw a light pencil line around top of table 2 inches from edge; divide center area into three equal sections and mark with pencil. Using ½-inch-wide foam brush and neutral grey, paint a ½-inch-wide line centered over each pencil line; let dry completely.

2 Apply ¼-inch-wide painter's tape over center of each painted line, pressing down firmly.

12 CLEAR UV PROTECTANT
This spray varnish by Krylon goes on smooth and dries to a very hard, durable finish that can stand up to daily use.

75 FAUX TILE
Apply stucco medium, using putty knife, to flatten surface unevenly. A second layer will give the illusion of flaked and chipped stone.

FAUX STONE TABLE

ASSEMBLY DIAGRAM

UNIQUE ENTRY TABLES CUTTING CHART (Actual Sizes)				
P	T	W	L	#
A	¾"	11"	23½"	1
B	¾"	3½"	8"	2
C	¾"	3½"	22"	2
D	1½"	1½"	24"	4
E	⅜"	1⅜"	5⅛"	2
F	⅜"	1⅜"	17½"	2

3 Paint table legs and tabletop outside taped area with mink tan, applying multiple coats to cover. Let dry.

4 Following manufacturer's directions, mix milk chocolate with glazing medium and use a dampened sea sponge to dab onto mink tan area of table top. Repeat process with antique white, then mink tan. Let dry.

5 Use putty knife to apply a layer of natural Stuccos to taped-off areas in center of tabletop, and to end and side boards; let dry. In same manner, apply a thin coat of light ecru Stuccos over first layer. Let dry completely.

6 Following manufacturer's directions, apply stain to stucco areas with paper towels, wiping off excess and leaving stain in crevices. Let dry.

7 Remove painter's tape. Sand stucco areas well and lightly sand edges of tabletop and legs to distress; remove dust. Mix titanium white with glazing medium and brush onto all stucco and sponged areas of table; let dry.

8 Apply two coats of satin varnish to entire table following manufacturer's directions. ❀

GRAND ENTRANCES

Designs by Patti J. Ryan

Attractive and functional, these style-conscious hall trees hold jackets, caps, bookbags and more.

PROJECT SIZE
22½x32½x4 inches

TOOLS
- Table saw or circular saw
- Large compass
- Saber saw
- Miter saw
- Drill
- Carpenter's square
- Nail set

SUPPLIES FOR ONE HALL TREE
- ⅜-inch plywood: 2x4-foot sheet
- Half-round molding: 5 feet
- ½x1¼-inch molding: 2 feet
- ⅜x⅜-inch mirror trim molding: 10 feet
- ½x½-inch molding: 4 feet
- Sandpaper: 180- and 220-grit
- Wood putty
- Crafter's Pick Sand-N-Stain wood glue from API
- Brads and finish nails
- Masking tape
- Four 8x12-inch mirrors
- Four 3½-inch white coat/hat hooks
- Four brass mini coat/hat hooks
- DecoArt Americana Primer & Stain Blocker #DSA34
- DecoArt gloss #DS19 DuraClear Varnish
- Hanging hardware
- Mirror adhesive

For Beach House Welcome Hall Tree
- DecoArt Americana acrylic paint: baby blue #DA42, Hauser light green #DA131, lavender #DA34, sapphire #DA99, baby pink #DA31 and titanium white #DA01
- Foam stamps: large fish, small fish, star fish, anchor
- Marvy Decocolor opaque paint markers: light green and white

For Antique Red Coat Rack
- Embossed wood appliqué
- DecoArt Americana glorious gold #DA071 Dazzling Metallics
- DecoArt Weathered Wood Crackling Medium #DAS8
- DecoArt Tuscany red #DSA13 Americana Satins

CUTTING

1 For back board, use table saw or circular saw to cut a 21½x32-inch piece from ⅜-inch plywood. Mark a line 4¼ inches from top edge; also, mark the board in half lengthwise.

2 Place large compass along the board's centerline; adjust position as needed to draw an arc that begins at the 4½-inch line on one side of the board, touches the top edge at the centerline, and ends at the 4½-inch point on the other side of the board. Use a saber saw to cut the arch.

3 Cut half-round molding into two 27-inch lengths for side trim.

4 Cut ½x1¼-inch molding into one 22½-inch length for bottom ledge.

5 Cut ⅜x⅜-inch mirror trim molding into one 21½-inch length for top horizontal trim. Set remaining length of mirror trim molding aside.

6 Cut ½x½-inch molding into two 8-inch lengths for horizontal mirror dividers, and one 24½-inch length for

BEACH HOUSE WELCOME

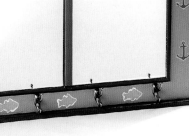

6 ACRYLIC PAINT

Water-based and non-toxic, Deco Art's Americana acrylic paint is an all-purpose paint for decorative painting, home decor and general craft painting for use on almost any surface.

17 SHAPED STAMPING

Use a purchased foam or sponge stamp with acrylic paint to place an image on your project. You can also make your own stamp from a sponge or piece of foam.

30 PURCHASED MOLDING

Wood molding is mitered at the corners and glued to the front of the frame for a decorative finish.

vertical mirror divider.

7 Sand all cut edges smooth.

ASSEMBLE

1 Fill imperfections in arch edge of back board with wood putty; let dry and sand smooth.

2 Position side trim on sides of back board flush with front and bottom edges. Drill six to eight pilot holes; glue and nail in place with brads.

3 Center bottom ledge on bottom of back board flush with back edge of board, forming a small ledge. *Note: Ledge will extend approximately ½ inch on each side. Drill five to six pilot holes; glue and nail in place with finish nails.*

4 Position top horizontal trim on 4¼-inch line. Drill pilot holes; glue and nail in place with brads.

5 Mark horizontal parallel lines ¾ inch and 12¾ inches below top

horizontal trim. Position vertical mirror divider on center line with top edge at ¾-inch mark. Position horizontal mirror dividers on 12¾-inch line on each side of vertical divider. Temporarily tape dividers in place.

6 *Note: Fold a piece of masking tape to form a tab at one edge of each mirror for ease in picking up mirrors.* Place one mirror in each section formed by dividers, positioning mirrors close to dividers. Cut and miter remaining length of ⅜x⅜-inch mirror trim molding to fit around outer dimensions of mirrors (approximately 16½ inches wide by 24½ inches long), allowing a little "wiggle room" so mirrors can be removed when painting the back board and moldings. Drill pilot holes and glue and nail mirror dividers with brads. Drill pilot holes and glue and attach mirror trim molding with brads. Remove mirrors and discard tape tabs.

7 Center large coat hooks on each side of mirrors 3½ inches and 16 inches from bottom edge of top horizontal trim; mark placement. Drill pilot holes.

8 Center small hooks between bottom mirror trim and bottom ledge, spacing 3½ inches apart; drill pilot holes.

9 Set nails. Fill nail holes with wood putty; let dry. Sand surfaces smooth and remove dust

Finishes

BEACH HOUSE WELCOME

1 Apply primer and stain blocker to all wood surfaces following manufacturer's directions. Paint as follows, applying multiple coats of paint as needed to cover, letting dry after each application:

Back board—Base-coat front and edges with *baby blue.*

Mirror dividers—Base-coat fronts with *Hauser light green,* and edges with *lavender.*

Mirror trim molding—Base-coat with *lavender.*

Bottom ledge and top horizontal trim—Base-coat with *sapphire.*

2 Referring to photo for placement, use compass to mark a ¼-inch-wide border on arch ½ inch from top edge and top horizontal trim. Paint a ¼-inch-wide border with Hauser light green; let dry.

3 Position large fish stamp in center of arch; mark lightly with pencil. Apply titanium white to stamp, then carefully press in place. Use a paintbrush to fill in any missed areas of white undercoat. Let dry. Clean stamp and let dry. Use paintbrush or sponge to randomly apply baby blue, Hauser light green, lavender, sapphire and baby pink to large fish stamp, then carefully

position over undercoat and press into place. Touch up as needed; let dry.

4 Randomly apply baby pink and titanium white to starfish stamp, then apply on either side of large fish. Reload stamp and apply on opposite side of fish. In same manner, stamp small fish image between small hook positions below mirror. Let dry.

5 Use Hauser light green to stamp two anchor images below each large hook position; let dry.

6 Outline and add detail to stamped images using white paint marker.

76 WOOD APPLIQUÉ
Attach a purchased embossed wood appliqué with regular wood glue, then paint or stain with the rest of the project.

77 CRACKLE FINISH
This easy, fast-drying, one-step process creates an antique look on wood, metal or any painted surface.

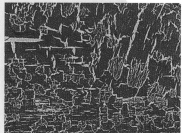

30 PURCHASED MOLDING
Wood molding is mitered at the corners and glued to the front of the frame for a decorative finish.

ANTIQUE RED COAT RACK

7 Apply a coat of gloss varnish to all painted surfaces, following manufacturer's directions.

8 Attach hooks. Attach hanging hardware to back. Following manufacturer's directions, apply mirror adhesive to back of each mirror, then press and hold in place. Allow adhesive to set up before moving.

ANTIQUE RED COAT RACK

1 Referring to photo for placement, position embossed wood appliqué in center of arch. Glue and clamp in place. Drill pilot holes and nail in place with brads.

2 Apply primer and stain blocker to all wood surfaces following manufacturer's directions. Base-coat all wood surfaces with glorious gold; let dry. Lightly wet-sand with 220-grit sandpaper and remove dust. Apply a second coat; let dry.

3 Following manufacturer's directions, apply a generous coat of Weathered Wood crackling medium in a crisscross pattern to all wood surfaces. When tacky, apply a top coat of Tuscany red. *Note: Do not re-stroke over an area; touch up any missed areas using a #4 round brush. Let dry thoroughly.*

4 Apply a coat of gloss varnish following manufacturer's directions.

5 Paint trim moldings and wood embellishments with glorious gold to highlight edges.

6 Attach hooks. Attach hanging hardware to back. Following manufacturer's directions, apply mirror adhesive to back of each mirror, then press and hold in place. Allow adhesive to set up before moving. ✸

TRUMEAU
MIRRORS

Designs by Patti J. Ryan

Originally a French architectural term, trumeau was being used by the mid-18th century to describe a mirror that was placed on a mantel shelf. Now, a trumeau mirror is characterized by its distinctive design, rather than where it is placed.

PROJECT SIZE
15x36x1 inches

TOOLS
- Table saw or circular saw
- Miter saw
- Drill
- Carpenter's square
- Nail set
- Clamps

SUPPLIES FOR ONE MIRROR
- ⅜-inch plywood: 2x4-foot sheet
- Half-round molding: 10 feet
- ½x½-inch molding: 4 feet
- ⅜x⅜-inch mirror trim molding: 7 feet
- Sandpaper: 180- and 220-grit
- Masking tape
- 12x24-inch mirror
- Crafter's Pick Sand-N-Stain wood glue from API
- Brads and finish nails
- Embossed wood appliqué
- Wood putty
- DecoArt Americana Primer & Stain Blocker #DSA34
- 12x6-inch art print
- Crafter's Pick The Ultimate! Glue from API
- Hanging hardware

- Mirror adhesive
- 12x24-inch mirror
- Cotton swabs and soft cotton cloths
- Paintbrushes

For Gilded Entry Mirror
- DecoArt Tuscany red #DSA13 Americana Satins
- Mona Lisa gold Leaf Adhesive Size: Fast-Track spray #010211
- Mona Lisa Genuine Gold Colour Imitation Metal Leaf #204
- Cotton swabs
- Soft cotton cloths
- DecoArt mahogany #AMS09 Americana Water-based Stain
- DecoArt gloss #DAS12 Americana Spray Sealer

For Blue Skies Entry Mirror
- DecoArt Americana Satins: evening blue #DSA16 and French blue #DSA43
- DecoArt shimmering silver Americana Dazzling Metallics
- DecoArt gloss #DSA27 Americana Satins varnish

CUTTING

1 For back board, use table saw or circular saw to cut a 15x36-inch piece from ⅜-inch plywood; sand edges smooth.

2 Cut and miter half-round molding to fit around outer edges of back board, flush with front edge; sand cut edges smooth. Drill pilot holes; glue and nail in place with finish nails.

3 Mark position of art print by drawing horizontal lines 2½ and 8½ inches from top edge of trimmed back board; draw vertical lines 1½ inches from each side to form a 12x6-inch rectangle. Cut and miter ½x½-inch trim molding to fit around rectangle. Sand cut edges smooth.

4 Mark position of mirror by drawing horizontal lines 9½ inches from top edge and 2½ inches from bottom edge; draw vertical lines 1½ inches from each side to form a 12x24-inch rectangle. *Note: Fold a piece of masking tape to form a tab at one edge of mirror for ease in positioning mirror. Position mirror; adjust marks as needed. Cut and miter ⅜x⅜-inch mirror trim molding to fit around mirror, allowing slight space so mirror can be removed when painting.*

SPOOL CABINET DUET

Design by Anna Thompson

These beautiful and functional cabinets add a touch of yesteryear to your home. Use them for sewing or craft supplies, jewelry, scarves or other small items.

CUTTING

1 Cut 1x12 to a 48-inch length; rip to 10¼-inch width. Cut one 20-inch length (D) for bottom and one 19¼-inch length (E) for top. Using router and ⅜-inch roundover bit, round both sides of all four edges of top and bottom, to create a "bullnose" edge.

2 Cut remaining 1x12 to a 24-inch length; rip to 8¾-inch width. Using router with ⅜-inch rabbeting bit, cut a ⅜x⅜-inch rabbet along one edge of 8¾x24-inch board. With rabbeted edge facing down, use router with ⅜-inch roundover bit to round front outside edge only of 8¾x24-inch board. Cut board to two 9⅛-inch lengths (A) for ends.

3 From ⅜-inch beadboard plywood, cut a 17¼x9⅛-inch piece (C) for back.

4 Cut ¾x3-inch white pine to three 17¼-inch lengths (I) for drawer fronts.

5 Using table saw, or router with an edge guide, cut a ¼-inch-wide dado ¼-inch deep ½ inch from one long edge of 12-foot ½x2½-inch white pine. Cut six 15½-inch lengths (H) for drawer backs and auxiliary fronts, and six 8-inch lengths (G) for drawer sides.

6 From ¼-inch birch plywood, cut three 8x16-inch lengths (F) for drawer bottoms.

7 Cut ½x½-inch white pine to four 8-inch lengths (B) for drawer runners. Predrill a ⅛-inch hole on the end of each runner; countersink so ¾-inch screw shank will fall through the hole.

ASSEMBLE

1 On inside of each cabinet end (A), position one drawer runner (B) 2⅝ inches from bottom edge with back of runners flush with rabbet on back edge; screw in place using ¾-inch screws. Position and attach remaining two drawer runners in same manner 2⅝ inches above first two runners.

PROJECT SIZE
20x10½x10¼ inches

TOOLS
- Table saw or circular saw
- Cordless drill
- Orbital sander
- Router with ⅜-inch rabbeting bit, ⅜-inch roundover bit and 45-degree bevel bit
- Drill with ¼-inch bit, and ⅜-inch countersink and ⅛-inch predrill bit

SUPPLIES FOR ONE CABINET
- 1x12 No. 2 grade white pine: 8 feet
- ⅜-inch beadboard plywood: 2x2 feet
- ¾x3-inch No. 2 grade white pine*: 6 feet
- ½ x 2½-inch white pine*: 12 feet
- ¼-inch plywood: 2x2 feet
- ½ x ½-inch No. 2 grade white pine*: 3 feet
- 1⅝-inch wood screws
- 1-inch wood screws
- ¾-inch wood screws
- ⅜-inch flush maple plugs
- Wood glue
- 1-inch brads
- Double-sided carpet tape
- Six 1-inch wooden knobs with screws
- 0000 steel wool

For Classic Cabinet
- Orange shellac flakes
- Denatured alcohol
- Soft, fine-bristle brush
- Mason jar with lid

For Old-Time Cabinet
- Dark liquid stain
- Black satin paint
- Finishing brushes
- Stencil
- Acrylic paint in desired colors
- Dark brown paste wax

Measurements given are actual, not nominal. Standard nominal lumber will need to be ripped to size.

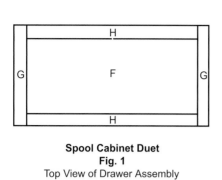

Spool Cabinet Duet
Fig. 1
Top View of Drawer Assembly

P	T	W	L	#
A	¾"	8¾"	9⅛"	2
B	½"	½"	8"	4
C	⅜"	17¼"	9⅛"	1
D	¾"	10¼"	20"	1
E	¾"	10¼"	19¼"	1
F	¼"	8"	16"	3
G	½"	2½"	8"	6
H	½"	2½"	15½"	6
I	¾"	3"	17¼"	3

SPOOL CABINET
DUET
CUTTING CHART
(Actual Sizes)

ASSEMBLY
DIAGRAM

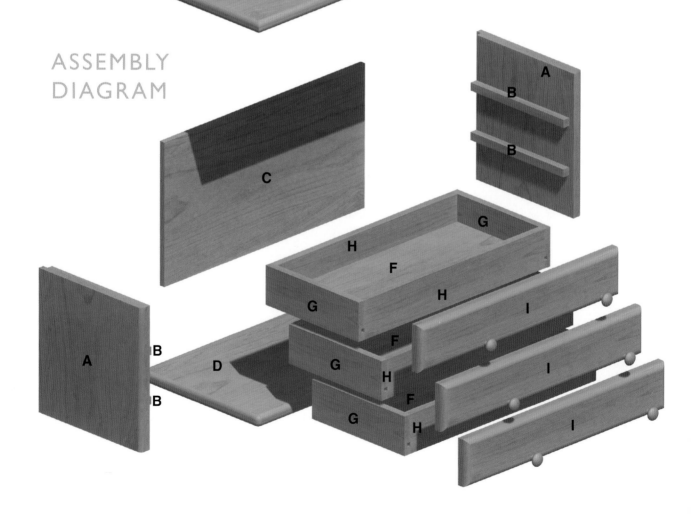

2 Referring to assembly diagram, glue and nail back (C) to ends (A), keeping top edges flush. Positioning sides 1 inch from ends and ⅜ inch from back edge, attach bottom (D) to sides using 1⅝-inch screws. ***Note:*** *Predrill screws and countersink screws to accept ⅜-inch flush plugs.*

3 Position top (E) so sides are ¾ inch from ends of top and ⅜ inch from back. Predrill and attach to sides with screws in same manner as for bottom.

4 Slide short edges of drawer bottoms (F) into dadoes on drawer sides (G), then slide long edges of drawer bottoms into dadoes on backs and auxiliary fronts (H). Glue and nail ends together, forming butt joints (Fig. 1).

5 Slide drawers in place in cabinet. Position and attach drawer fronts (I) to auxiliary fronts of drawers. ***Note:*** *Drawer fronts should not touch each other, or top and bottom of cabinet.* Attach drawer fronts from

inside each drawer using two 1-inch screws at each end of the drawer. Drill ¼-inch holes centered 3 inches from ends of drawer fronts; attach knobs with screws provided.

Finishes
CLASSIC CABINET

1 Mix 2 ounces orange shellac flakes in 8 ounces of denatured alcohol; allow flakes to dissolve approximately two hours, stirring frequently.

CLASSIC CABINET

80 **SHELLAC WASH**
Dissolve shellac flakes in denatured alcohol for a child-safe sealer that has no unpleasant or toxic fumes.

OLD-TIME CABINET

81 **STENCIL**
Use a purchased stencil to create a delicate look without being an expert painter.

2 Apply dissolved flakes with long strokes using a soft, fine-bristle brush and trying not to overlap strokes. (This would result in a darker color that is hard to blend in.)

3 Allow first coat to dry completely, then apply a second coat. **Note:** *It will look rather thick at this point. Steel wool briskly in a circular motion, then finish up by going with the grain.*

4 Apply as many coats as desired, using steel wool after each coat. Clean brush with denatured alcohol.

OLD-TIME CABINET

1 Following manufacturer's directions, apply dark liquid stain to cabinet; let dry thoroughly. Paint with black paint; let dry.

2 Steel wool painted surface to even out brush marks, then apply a second coat. Let dry.

3 Position stencil and paint with acrylic paint. Let dry. Use steel wool to remove some of the stencil design, allowing the dark finish to show through. ❈

SERENDIPITY
TABLES

Design by Wayne and Rhonda Sutter

Double your storage space with these space-saving sets! Use the larger round table next to a chair or sofa, then simply slide out the wedge-shaped pie table when more space is needed.

PROJECT NOTES

This project requires intermediate to advanced woodworking skill. Round table parts are indicated by RT and pie table parts are indicated by PT throughout.

CUTTING, DRILLING & PRELIMINARY ASSEMBLY

Tabletops

1 From 1x4 oak, use miter saw to cut eight 30-inch lengths for RT top (G), and six 22-inch lengths for PT top (L).

2 Cover flat work surfaces with visquene to protect surface and prevent project from adhering to surface. Lay out tabletop pieces for each table, being sure grain alternates on boards. For example, if the grain on the end of the first piece curves up, turn the second piece so the grain curves down, etc.

3 With ends flush, glue and clamp edges of boards together. ***Note:*** *Make sure tabletops are flat on the surface of the work area, that the visquene did not get pinched in the joints, and that all pieces stay flat as you tighten the clamps.* Let dry.

4 Sand entire surface of glued boards, tops and bottoms, to remove glue. Cut as follows:

PROJECT SIZE

Round Table: 28x26⅜x28 inches
Pie Table: 21x25x21 inches

TOOLS

- Miter saw
- Four or five clamps with a minimum 28-inch bite
- Pencil with 30-inch-long string or large compass
- Trammel points (optional)
- 24-inch-long straight edge
- Jigsaw
- Router with ¼-inch roundover over bit, ¼-inch straight bit (optional) and Chamfer bit (optional)
- Random orbital sander or hand sander
- Table saw
- Kreg pocket hole jig and bit
- Block plane or sharp chisel
- Drill with Phillips driver and ¹⁄₁₆- and ⅜-inch brad point bits

SUPPLIES FOR ONE EACH ROUND AND PIE TABLE

- 1x4 oak: three 8-foot lengths and one 10-foot length
- 1x6 oak: two 8-foot lengths
- ¼x8-inch oak*: two 4-foot lengths
- ¼x2-inch oak*: 2 feet
- Visquene or waxed paper: 30x30 inches and 24x24 inches
- Wood glue
- Twenty-eight 1¼-inch pocket screws
- Four 1-inch pocket screws
- 32 oak pocket-hole plugs
- Six 2-inch coarse-thread drywall screws
- Six ⅜-inch oak flat wood plugs
- 4d finish nails

For Night & Day Round Table
- Minwax Oil Stain
- Zinsser Bull's Eye Shellac
- Alcohol

For Night & Day Pie Table
- Bartley Paste Wood Filler
- Minwax Oil Stain
- Naptha
- Stiff bristled brush
- Burlap

For Cherry Round Table
- Swing Paints Circa 1850 Tung Oil

For Cherry Pie Table
- Swing Paints Circa 1850 Tung N Teak Oil

For Oak Round Table
- Swing Paints Circa 1850 Antique Oil

For Oak Pie Table
- Swing Paints Circa 1850 Antique Paste Varnish
- Lint-free cloth

*Measurements given are actual, not nominal. Standard nominal lumber will need to be ripped to size.

Round table—Measure and mark the center width of glued boards (G). If it is less than 28 inches, that is the measurement you will use for your diameter. If it is 28 inches or greater, use a 28-inch diameter. Measure the length of the glued boards and lightly mark the center to intersect with the center width mark. Use large compass, tramel points or pencil with string to mark cut lines, using center mark as pivot point. **Note:** *If using pencil and string, tie string to pencil. Divide diameter in half and mark that distance from the pencil on the string. Hold the mark on the string at the pivot point and mark cut lines, keeping string taught. Make sure the string mark and the center mark stay together.* Check lines, then cut with jigsaw. If hand sanding, sand the flat edge of the tabletop.

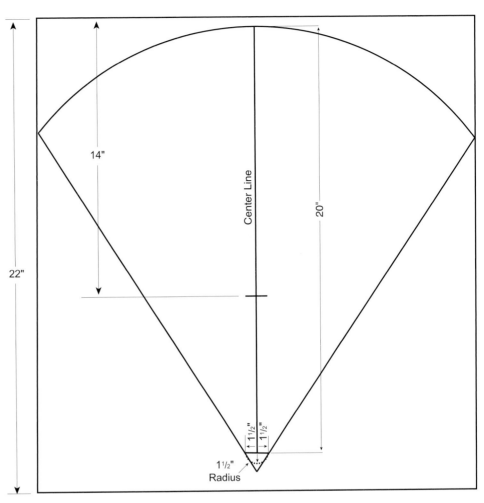

Serendipity Tables
Pie Tabletop Cutting Diagram
Fig. 1

Pie table—Decide which side of glued boards (L) will be the top; turn face down to mark and cut it. Measure with the grain 14 inches from the end and mark; measure width and lightly mark the center to intersect the first mark. Using compass or pencil with string (see instructions for round table) mark an arc, using marks as the pivot point. Make a mark indicating the center at the crest of the arc just drawn. Use a straight edge to lightly draw a line joining both center marks. **Note:** *This line should run with the grain.* Measure from the crest of the arc along the center line 20 inches; measure 1½ inches to the left and to the right of (perpendicu-

lar to) the center line and make a mark even with the 20-inch mark. From these marks, use the straight edge to draw cut lines to the left and right ends of the arc respectively (Fig. 1) to form the pie shape. From the center mark (20 inches from the top arc) set the compass at 1½ inches; mark a semicircle to finish the point of the pie. Round the points of the arc at the wide end of the pie shape. Cut arcs and sides with a jig saw. If hand sanding, sand the flat edge of the top.

5 Rout top and bottom edges of both tabletops using ¼-inch roundover bit. Sand smooth with the random orbit

sander, or hand sand again, being sure to work with the grain of the wood.

Legs & rails

1 From one 1x6 oak board, use miter saw to cut one 25-inch length, one 24-inch length and one 17-inch length. (Set remaining 30-inch length aside for use in step 2.) From second 1x6 oak board, use miter saw to cut one 17-inch length, one 12-inch length, one 10¾-inch length and one 25-inch length (Set the remainder of this second 1x6 aside for future projects.)

2 Using table saw, rip one of the 25-inch lengths and the remaining 30-

SELECTING WOOD FOR THE TABLETOPS

The tops of these tables are made from solid wood 1x4s that are glued together. Here are some things to consider as you look for materials:

• If you use 1x10s (actual ¾x9¼ inches), three pieces glued together will give the diameter needed for the round table, and the look of the tabletop may be very uniform, almost giving the appearance of being one solid piece. However, as the wood ages, it may warp slightly.

• If you use 1x4s (actual ¾x3½ inches), it will take eight pieces to obtain the needed diameter of the round table. Narrower boards may also be used, giving the tabletop a more butcher-block appearance. With these options, the chances of warping are minimal.

• You may consider anything from the actual 9¼ inches of a 1x10, to ripping pieces as narrow as 1 inch. Whatever you do, be consistent, using the same board widths for both tables.

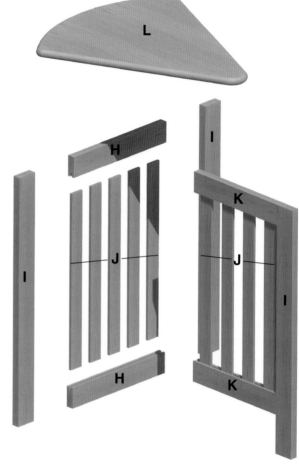

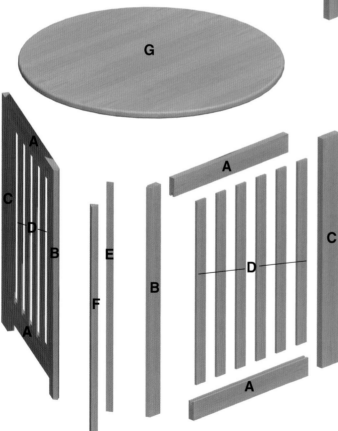

SERENDIPITY TABLES CUTTING CHART
(Actual Sizes)

P	T	W	L	#
A	¾"	2"	17"	4
B	¾"	2½"	30"	2
C	¾"	2½"	25"	2
D	¼"	1⅜"	20"	12
E	¾"	⅛"	25"	1
F	¾"	1"	25"	1
G	¾"	3½"	30"	8
H	¾"	2"	12"	2
I	¾"	2"	24"	3
J	¼"	1⅜"	17"	9
K	¾"	2"	10¾"	2
L	¾"	3½"	22"	6

Undersides of round (top) and pie (bottom) tables

inch length (step 1) into two 2½-inch widths, making two 25-inch-long RT legs (C) and two 30-inch-long RT legs (B). Adjust table saw and rip a 2-inch width from the second 25-inch length. (Remainder of board will be used for making the spline in a later step.) Use miter saw to trim 2-inch-wide piece to

24-inch length for one PT leg (I). Rip 24-inch length cut in step 1 into two 2-inch widths to make two more PT legs (I).

3 Rip each of the remaining lengths cut in step 1 into 2-inch widths: two 17-inch lengths (A) for RT rails, one

12-inch length (H) for PT rails, and one 10¾-inch length(K) for PT rails.

4 Reset table saw so blade will make a ⅜-inch high cut, and the distance between the fence and the edge of the blade closest to the fence is ¼ inch. Make a pass over the table saw blade with a rail piece, then turn that piece around (so the opposite side is against the fence and the same edge is being cut). Make a second pass right next to the first, cutting a groove into the rail that is ¼-inch wide. ***Note:*** *If you have a router table, you may prefer to set the ¼-inch straight bit to make a cut ⅜-inch deep and cut right down the center of the rails. Repeat for all rail pieces,*

NIGHT & DAY ROUND AND PIE TABLES

2 Using miter saw, cut the 1⅜-inch strips into twelve 20-inch lengths (D) for RT slats, and nine 17-inch lengths (J) for PT slats.

Spline and leg joints

Note: Steps 1–4 are a challenge for even the intermediate woodworker. If you want to see how you do, practice on a piece of scrap wood first, such as a 1x6 No. 2 white pine ripped to 2½ inches. If you have any reservations at all, take it to your local lumberyard and have it milled for you.

1 From the 25-inch length remaining from step 2 of legs and rails, use table saw to rip a ¾x⅛x25-inch piece (E) for spline, and a ¾x1x25-inch piece (F) for joint cover.

2 For joint cover (F), bevel the sides of remaining 25-inch length (step 1 of spline and leg joints) at a 30-degree angle as follows (Finished piece will be a triangular shape):

Rip No. 1—Set the fence so the blade cuts right at the edge of the board.

Rip No. 2—Move the fence ¹³⁄₁₆-inches closer to the blade and turn the board over so same side of board is still on the fence. *Note: Use a leftover piece of wood to push pieces through the table saw. Don't risk you fingers!*

cutting a groove on one side of rail only. You should end up with four 17-inch RT rails (A), two 12-inch PT rails (H) and two 10¾-inch PT rails (K).

5 On one side of each rail, use pocket hole jig to drill two holes at each end.

Slats

1 Adjust table saw to rip both ¼x 8-inch lengths and the ¼x2-inch lengths into 1⅜-inch-wide strips.

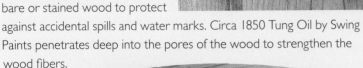

84 TUNG OIL

Apply this finish onto bare or stained wood to protect against accidental spills and water marks. Circa 1850 Tung Oil by Swing Paints penetrates deep into the pores of the wood to strengthen the wood fibers.

85 TUNG N TEAK OIL

Ideal for interior and exterior use, this finish provides a low-luster, hand rubbed finish on bare or stained wood. Circa 1850 Tung N Teak Oil by Swing Paints combines the penetration of teak oil with the durability of tung oil to strengthen the wood fibers.

CHERRY ROUND & PIE TABLES

3 Chamfer (bevel) the two 30-inch-long RT legs (B) with a 30-degree angle set on the table saw, or use the router with a chamfer bit (optional). If using the table saw, screw a 30-inch piece of stock wood to the leg piece, driving the screws through the stock piece first at each end, making sure there are at least 25 inches between the screws. Measure the thickness of the stock piece and set the table saw fence that distance from the blade. Rip the chamfer. **Note:** *The chamfer leg will be perpendicular to the table saw deck. Whatever cuts you make to one leg, do to the other leg at the same time. Remove stock piece.*

4 With the blade still set at 30 degrees, cut a spline slot in the same position on both chamfered legs. **Note:** *This slot should be ⅜-inch deep, perpendicular to the chamfered edge. The spline slot will allow the two chamfered pieces to be glued together at exactly the same point.* Lower the blade to ⅜-inch above the deck of the table saw. Set the fence so this cut is just past the beginning of the bevel, but not too close to the point.

5 Raise the table saw blade and cut the pointed end off the chamfered leg so there is exactly ½ inch at the width of the cut, perpendicular to the chamfer, and parallel to the spline slot.

6 Use the miter saw to cut the chamfered legs to 25 inches, making sure to cut enough off of each end to remove the screw holes left from step 3.

ASSEMBLE
Round table

1 Join one 17-inch RT rail (A) to one of the chamfered legs (B) and one of the straight legs (C). Make sure the side with the pocket holes is the same side as the bevel cut on the table leg. With the top of the rail flush with the tops of the legs, attach with glue and two 1¼-inch pocket screws each.

2 Insert six RT slats (D) into groove on rail; bump one slat up against the leg, then space the others evenly. Slip another rail (A) over bottoms of slats, securing slats with a drop of glue in the groove of the rail. **Note:** *Make sure the side of the rail with the pocket holes is on the same side as the bevel cut on the chamfered leg. Secure bottom rail to legs with glue and pocket screws. Glue pocket hole plugs into pocket holes;*

86 ANTIQUE OIL

Use this finish on all interior wood surfaces including paneling, woodwork, hardwood floors and furniture to guard against spills and stains. Circa 1850 Antique Oil by Swing Paints can be applied to bare, stained or finished wood to protect and restore old, tired finishes.

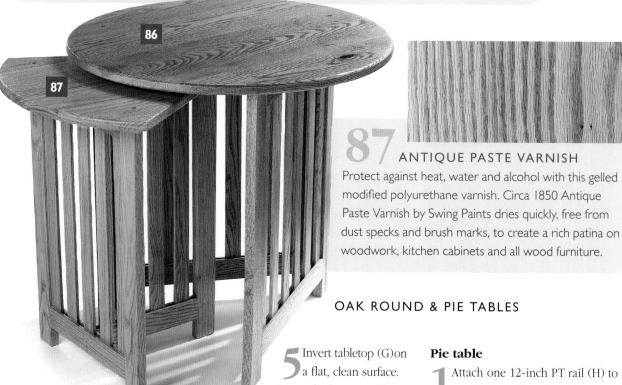

87 ANTIQUE PASTE VARNISH

Protect against heat, water and alcohol with this gelled modified polyurethane varnish. Circa 1850 Antique Paste Varnish by Swing Paints dries quickly, free from dust specks and brush marks, to create a rich patina on woodwork, kitchen cabinets and all wood furniture.

OAK ROUND & PIE TABLES

pare excess wood with a block plane or sharp chisel, then sand flush.

3 Repeat steps 1 and 2 for remaining RT leg, using remaining two 17-inch RT rails (A), remaining RT legs (B) and two remaining RT legs (C).

4 Run a bead of glue in each spline groove and along the chamfered edge; insert the spline (E) and join the two chamfered legs. Glue joint cover (F) in place, wrapping with masking tape around leg to secure the three pieces until dry. Remove tape and sand edges flush with table leg.

5 Invert tabletop (G) on a flat, clean surface. Center the leg assembly on the underside of the tabletop; mark the position of each leg. Remove legs. Mark the center point of each leg position and drill a ¹⁄₁₆-inch pilot hole through table top at these points.

6 Turn tabletop over and drill a ³⁄₈-inch hole ³⁄₈-inch deep where each ¹⁄₁₆-inch pilot hole comes through. Place the top back on the legs, lining legs up with marks made earlier, and use a 4d finish nail through the pilot holes to mark the predrill points. Remove tabletop and drill into legs at the nail marks. Run a bead of glue along the leg top; reset the tabletop and secure it to the legs with three 2-inch screws. Insert ³⁄₈-inch flat hole plugs and sand flush.

Pie table

1 Attach one 12-inch PT rail (H) to two PT legs (I) with pocket screws, making sure tops are flush and groove on rail is facing down. Slip five PT slats (J) into groove on rail; position one slat next to each leg and the rest evenly spaced between. Slip another 12-inch PT rail (H) over bottoms of slats, securing slats with a drop of glue in the groove of the rail. Attach lower rail to legs with pocket screws. Insert pocket plugs and sand smooth.

2 In same manner, fasten one 10¾-inch PT rail (K) to remaining PT leg (I) using 1¼-inch pocket screws and to center of upper rail of assembled unit using 1-inch pocket screws. Make sure tops are flush and groove on rail is facing down. Slip remaining four PT slats

(J) into groove on rail and position as in step 1. Slip remaining 10¾-inch PT rail (K) over bottoms of slats, securing slats with a drop of glue in the groove of the rail. Attach lower rail to leg and assembled unit with pocket screws. Install pocket hole plugs and sand flush.

3 Invert pie tabletop (L) on a flat, clean surface. Center the leg assembly on the underside of the tabletop; mark the position of each leg. Remove legs. Mark the center point of each leg position and drill a ¹⁄₁₆-inch pilot hole through table top at these points.

4 Turn tabletop over and drill a ⅜-inch hole ⅜-inch deep where each ¹⁄₁₆-inch pilot hole comes through. Place the top back on the legs, lining legs up with marks made earlier, and use a 4d finish nail through the pilot holes to mark the predrill points. Remove tabletop and drill into legs at the nail marks. Run a bead of glue along the leg top; reset the tabletop and secure it to the legs with three 2-inch screws. Insert ⅜-inch flat hole plugs and sand flush.

Finishes

NIGHT & DAY ROUND TABLE

1 Sand to obtain a smooth, uniform surface; remove dust.

2 Apply stain with a brush or cloth. Wait 10 minutes then wipe off excess. Apply a second coat after 12 hours. Let dry for 24 hours before applying shellac.

3 Flood the shellac liberally onto the wood, letting it soak into any end grain areas until the wood stops absorbing the shellac. Wipe off any excess with a cloth dampened with alcohol.

4 Let dry 20 minutes. Sand lightly and remove dust before additional coats are applied.

NIGHT AND DAY PIE TABLE

1 Sand carefully to at least 220 grit to obtain a smooth, uniform surface; remove all dust.

2 Thin wood filler with naptha to the consistency of thick cream. Apply filler liberally in any direction with a stiff-bristled brush, working it into the pores of the wood with the brush.

3 Immediately after brushing, remove excess filler at a 45 degree angle to the grain. After scraping, wait for filler to haze over, about five to 20 minutes.

4 Using a piece of burlap, start rubbing the excess filler off the surface across the grain. Continue rubbing until no filler appears on the burlap.

5 Switch to a clean piece of burlap and rub in a figure-eight pattern.

6 Let filler dry at least 12 hours, then sand lightly.

7 Apply Oil Stain with a brush or cloth. Wait 10 minutes then wipe off excess. Apply a second coat after 12 hours.

CHERRY ROUND TABLE

1 Sand to obtain a smooth, uniform surface; remove dust.

2 Rub a liberal amount of Tung Oil onto the surface with bare hand or lint-free cloth. Wipe off excess and allow to dry for one hour.

3 Apply a second coat as above, wipe off and allow to dry.

CHERRY PIE TABLE

1 Sand to obtain a smooth, uniform surface; remove dust.

2 Rub a liberal amount of Tung'n Teak Oil onto the surface with bare hand or lint-free cloth. Wipe off excess and allow to dry for one hour.

3 Apply a second coat as above, wipe off excess and allow to dry.

OAK ROUND TABLE

1 Sand to obtain a smooth, uniform surface; remove dust.

2 Wipe on a liberal amount of Antique Oil using a lint-free cloth. Buff evenly with long strokes in the direction of the grain until the oil is absorbed by the wood.

3 If desired, apply a second coat after 24 hours.

OAK PIE TABLE

1 Sand to obtain a smooth, uniform surface; remove dust.

2 With a lint-free cloth, spread a thin layer of Paste Varnish over the surface. Rub evenly in the direction of the grain.

3 Wait eight hours, then smooth lightly with extra fine steel wool.

4 Using a cloth slightly dampened with Paste Varnish, rub lightly with quick, full-length strokes in the direction of the grain. Continue until there is no drag on the cloth and the surface is smooth. ✽

SHOW OFF
SHELVES

Designs by Anna Thompson

Display cherished collectibles or framed family photos with a set of wall shelves for any room in your home. Choose the formal beauty of cherry stain or the casual look of antique country.

CUTTING

Note: Use table saw to rip width. Use miter saw to cut length.

1 Rip 1x8 to 6-inch width; cut length to 24 inches for top board.

PROJECT SIZE
24x24¾x6 inches

TOOLS
- Table saw
- Router with ¾-inch straight bit
- Scroll saw
- Miter saw
- Clamps capable of spanning 0–24 inches
- Drill with ⅛- and ⅜-inch bits
- Phillips head driver

SUPPLIES FOR ONE SHELF
- 1x8: 3 feet
- 1x6: 8 feet
- ¼x24x24-inch* beadboard panel (for crackle shelf)
- ¼x24x24-inch* cherry plywood (for cherry shelf)

- Sandpaper
- Flat Phillips head screws: eight #6x1½-inch (depending on dado fit, step 8), four #6x2-inch, four #6x1-inch and four #4x1-inch
- Wood glue
- ⅜-inch flush plugs

Measurements given are actual, not nominal. Standard nominal lumber will need to be ripped to size.

For Beadboard Display Shelf
- Maroon semigloss wall paint
- Crackle medium
- White semigloss wall paint

For Cherry Display Shelf
- Natural Danish oil finish by Deft
- Paint roller and pan
- Soft cloths
- Furniture wax

2 From 1x6, cut one 49-inch and one 47-inch length. Rip the 49-inch length to 5-inch width; cut two 24-inch lengths (for sides). Rip the 47-inch length to 4¾-inch width; cut two 21-inch lengths for shelves.

3 Set router to cut a ¼-inch-wide and ⅜-inch-deep rabbet along the back edges of sides and top. *Note: Use ripped edges for back edges.*

4 Stack sides with ends flush and rabbeted edges on the same side; clamp together. If lengths are uneven, trim longer board. Transfer decorative end pattern to lower edge of sides on top board; cut with scroll saw. Sand smooth.

5 Check shelves for length. If uneven, clamp together and trim flush using miter saw.

6 On inside of each side board, measure and mark 8⅝ inches and 18½ inches from top. These points will be the centers of the shelf dados.

7 Place both side boards in jig (see instructions page 132) side-by-side, butting rabbeted edges together and making sure ends are flush. Match dado marks on side boards with ink marks on jig. Set router with ¾-inch straight

Jig Assembly

SUPPLIES

- ¾x13x18-inch AC plywood (for base)
- 1x2: two 18-inch lengths (A) and two 13-inch lengths (B)
- Twelve #6x1⅝-inch course-thread drywall screws

INSTRUCTIONS

1 Place one 18-inch 1x2 (A) flush along each 18-inch edge of plywood base for stops and clamp in place; drive in four screws evenly spaced from underside. Remove clamps.

2 Place one 13-inch 1x2 (B) on top of and perpendicular to the stops flush with right edge of base for router guide. *Note: It is essential that router tracks are perpendicular to stops; check angle with square. Predrill holes and secure with one screw at each end.*

3 Measure width of router base and use this measurement for the distance between router guides; position second router guide (B) and screw into place.

4 Measure from the center of router bit to the edge of the router base. Measure the same distance from the inside edge of either router guide and make a mark in ink. This will be the edge of your router cut and, in this case, the top edge of the dado. *Note: Check bottom of jig and make sure there are no screws in line with this mark. Side boards should fit snugly between stops.*

bit at a depth of ⁵⁄₁₆ inch and cut first dado in side boards, cutting through sides of jig. Move board to align second dado mark with edge of router cut on jig (the same side as the initial ink mark) and cut the second dado.

ASSEMBLE

1 Dry-fit shelves into dadoes. If fit is snug, remove shelves and apply glue in dadoes; refit and clamp shelves in place, making sure shelves are flush with front edges and rabbeted back edge. If fit is loose, glue and clamp shelves in place; predrill two holes through side boards into end of each shelf and secure with 1½-inch screws. *Note: To predrill holes, drill a ³⁄₈-inch-deep hole using ³⁄₈-inch bit, then drill through center of ³⁄₈-inch hole using ⅛-inch bit. This will allow a ³⁄₈-inch flush plug to cover the screw heads.* Wipe off excess glue with a damp cloth; let dry.

2 Measure the outside width of assembled shelf unit. Measure the full length of the top piece. Subtract the shelf unit measurement from the top measurement, and divide by two to determine how much the top will hang over the sides. Measure and mark overhang on underside of top piece.

3 Apply a small bead of glue along top edges of sides; place shelf unit on its back and clamp top piece in position. Predrill two holes through top into each side and secure with 2-inch screws. Wipe off excess glue; let dry.

4 Turn unit face down. Measure width and length of rabbeted

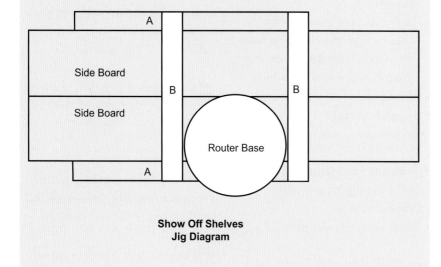

**Show Off Shelves
Jig Diagram**

area and subtract ⅛ inch from each. Cut plywood/beadboard to these measurements for shelf back.

5 Using ⅛-inch bit, predrill two holes evenly spaced into each shelf (about ⅓ of the way in from each side) and secure back to shelves with #6x1-inch screws. At a slight angle, drill a hole into rabbets at each corner and drive in #4x1-inch screws.

Finishes

BEADBOARD DISPLAY SHELF

1 Paint shelf with maroon semigloss wall paint following manufacturer's directions. Let dry.

2 Apply a thick coat of crackle medium and let dry until tacky.

3 Apply white semigloss wall paint over crackle coat and let dry.

CHERRY DISPLAY SHELF

1 Following manufacturer's directions, flood surface with natural Danish oil finish, using a paint roller drenched in the oil. Keep wet for 30 minutes, applying oil wherever the surface appears to be dry.

2 Wipe off excess oil with soft cloths. Let dry two hours. Repeat process twice.

3 Apply a light coat of furniture wax following manufacturer's directions. ✹

HELPFUL TIPS

• When ripping board widths, keep in mind that the greater the number of teeth on a saw blade, the smoother the cuts will be. An edge cut with a blade having 12 or fewer teeth may require sanding. If planing the edge to smooth it, be sure to allow a little extra width in the initial rip so the board width after planing is the appropriate width. Another option is to make sure the edge you cut is toward the back of the cabinet. This way, you save the sanding or planing, and the cabinet back (or the wall) covers most of that cut edge.

• If choosing a stained finish, consider staining all the pieces after you have made all the cuts. This eliminates the problem of trying to get stain into every corner.

• Always remember: A normal electrically driven saw blade will take out approximately ⅛ inch of wood to make its cut (hence the sawdust). Therefore, if you want the cut board to be 24 inches long, be sure to cut on the proper side of the pencil line to assure accuracy. For example, if you have measured from the right side of the board, cut on the left side of the pencil mark, bringing the right side of your saw blade right along the line, barely removing it. If you have measured from the left side of the board, bring the saw blade along the right side against the line.

TERMS TO KNOW

Rip—Cutting lumber the long way, with the grain, usually cutting to width.

Cross-cut—Cutting lumber across the grain, usually cutting to length.

Dado—Groove.

Rabbet—Notch.

Jig—A tool allowing you to make more than one identical cut, ensuring precision.

**Show Off Shelves
Decorative End**

CHERRY DISPLAY SHELF

1 DANISH OIL
For a beautiful and long-lasting oil finish, remember the old adage: Oil once a day for a week, once a week for a month, once a month for a year and every year thereafter.

BEADBOARD DISPLAY SHELF

77 CRACKLE FINISH
DecoArt's two-step crackle medium dries clear and can be antiqued for an aged look. Apply light, even coats for tiny cracks, or two to three heavy coats for large cracks.

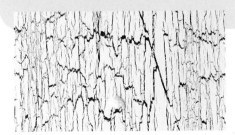

TRENDY
TRAYS

Designs by Patti J. Ryan

Whether you use them as game boards or serving pieces, these trays will be a welcome addition to your home.

CUTTING

1 Using table saw or circular saw, cut a 14x18-inch piece from ¼-inch birch plywood for tray bottom.

2 Cut ½x1½-inch stock into two 20-inch lengths for tray sides, and two 15-inch lengths for tray ends, cutting 20-inch length from each piece first. On 1½-inch-wide side of each length, lightly mark the center down the length of each piece. Use table saw to cut a ⁵⁄₁₆-inch groove ¼-inch deep along each mark.

3 Use miter saw to cut ends and sides to fit around tray bottom, fitting tray bottom into grooves. *Notes: Inside dimensions should be 17¾ inches for sides and 13⅝ inches for ends. Outer dimensions should be 18¾ inches for sides and 14½ inches for ends.*

ASSEMBLE

1 Dry-fit tray bottom, ends and sides together. *Note: Tray bottom should float snugly in grooves.* Disassemble tray. Sand all cut edges with 150- then 180-grit sandpaper; remove dust.

2 Reassemble tray, aligning mitered corners. Drill one or two pilot holes in each corner. Apply glue to miter joints. Align corners and check that tray is square, then secure with finish nails or brads. *Note: Do not glue tray bottom in grooves.*

3 Set nails; fill holes with wood putty and let dry. Sand sides and ends with 220-grit sandpaper; remove dust.

Finishes

GAME BOARD TRAY

1 Following manufacturer's directions, apply wood stain conditioner to tray; let dry, then lightly sand with 220-grit sandpaper and remove dust.

PROJECT SIZE
14½x18¾x1½ inches

TOOLS
- Table saw or circular saw
- Miter saw
- Drill
- Carpenter's square
- Nail set

For Game Board Tray
- Straight edge and scribing tool

SUPPLIES FOR ONE TRAY
- ¼x16x20-inch sheet birch plywood
- ½x1½-inch stock: two 36-inch lengths
- Finish nails or brads
- Wood putty
- Crafter's Pick Sand-N-Stain Glue from API
- Sandpaper: 150-, 180- and 220-grits
- 1-inch-wide painter's tape
- Clean, lint-free cloths
- Krylon gloss #7005 Polyurethane Clear Wood Finish Spray
- Four dome-shaped upholstery tacks
- Two drawer pulls

For Game Board Tray
- Graphite paper and stylus
- 1-inch-circle template
- DecoArt Americana Stain Conditioner #DSA33
- Small paintbrush
- DecoArt Americana Water-based Stain: maple #AMS07 and dark walnut #AMS11
- Minwax golden oak #210B Wood Finish Stain Marker
- Marvy Decocolor Markers: silver and gold

For Checkers (optional)
- DecoArt Americana Satins satin varnish #DSA28
- 36 inches 1-inch wooden dowel

For Leather Look Tray
- DecoArt Americana Primer and Stain Blocker #DSA34
- DecoArt Americana Satins: black #DSA25 and rustic red #DSA42
- DecoArt Americana Staining/ Antiquing Medium #DSA32
- Sea sponge
- DecoArt Americana Satins gloss varnish #DSA27
- Marvy copper Decocolor paint marker

GAME BOARD TRAY

88 METALLIC OUTLINES
Acid-free and nontoxic, these permanent paint markers from Uchida contain a lead-free, oil-based pigmented ink and have an extra fine-point for creating narrow outlines.

89 SCORED LINES
Use a scribing tool or nail with a straight edge to scribe the lines of the checkerboard. This will help keep the stain from bleeding into adjacent areas.

LEATHER LOOK TRAY

90 FAUX LEATHER WITH SPONGE
Use a natural sea sponge and acrylic paint mixed with glazing medium to achieve this leather-like appearance. Applying multiple layers of glaze gives depth to the finish.

2 Enlarge checkerboard pattern 153 percent; transfer to tray bottom using graphite paper and stylus. Using straight edge and scribing tool, score transfer lines for checkerboard. Use circle template and scribing tool to score circles. *Note: Scoring the lines will help prevent stain from bleeding to adjacent areas.*

3 Use painter's tape to mask outside edges of checkerboard, then mask off every other square inside checkerboard; burnish all edges. Use small paintbrush to apply dark walnut stain to exposed squares, following manufacturer's directions. Let dry. Remove tape. *Note: If stain has seeped under tape, lightly scrape away stain with the flat side of a utility knife blade.*

4 Mask checkerboard area with tape, leaving remainder of tray exposed; burnish edges. Following manufacturer's directions, apply maple stain to face and all sides of tray; let dry. Remove tape.

5 Use golden oak stain marker to darken the insides of circles; dab off stain with soft cloth, if needed.

6 Lightly sand all surfaces of tray with 220-grit sandpaper; remove dust.

7 Using paint markers and straight edge, outline checkerboard squares and outer edge of checkerboard with gold; add a silver outline around outer gold line.

8 Using circle template and paint markers, outline circles on one side of checkerboard with gold, and on other side with silver.

9 Spray tray with several light coats of Clear Wood Finish, following manufacturer's directions. Predrill a hole in bottom of each corner, then add upholstery tacks. Attach drawer pulls to tray ends, predrilling holes for screws.

Checkers (optional)

1 Use the miter saw to cut the 1-inch wooden dowel into twenty-four ⅜-inch-thick pieces. Sand smooth.

2 Apply stain conditioner to all surfaces of each checker, following manufacturer's directions. Apply dark walnut stain to 12 checkers.

3 Brush all 24 checkers with satin varnish; let dry.

LEATHER LOOK TRAY

1 Prime all surfaces with Primer and Stain Blocker; let dry. Lightly sand with 220-grit sandpaper and remove dust.

2 Apply two coats of black following manufacturer's directions; wet-sand lightly after each coat using 220-grit sandpaper. Wipe dry.

3 Use painter's tape to mask off a 1-inch border around edge of tray bottom and around centers of ends and sides. Burnish tape edges.

4 Mix a small amount of rustic red with an equal amount of staining/antiquing medium. Use a damp sea sponge to lightly dab mixture onto face of tray, rotating sponge and hand positions to create a random texture. Repeat on sides and ends of tray. Let dry. Remove tape.

5 Seal painted surface with a coat of satin varnish; let dry.

6 Using straight edge and copper paint marker, outline sponged areas on tray bottom and sides and ends of tray; let dry.

7 Spray tray with several light coats of Clear Wood Finish, following manufacturer's directions. Predrill a hole in bottom of each corner, then add upholstery tacks. Attach drawer pulls to tray ends, predrilling holes for screws. ✺

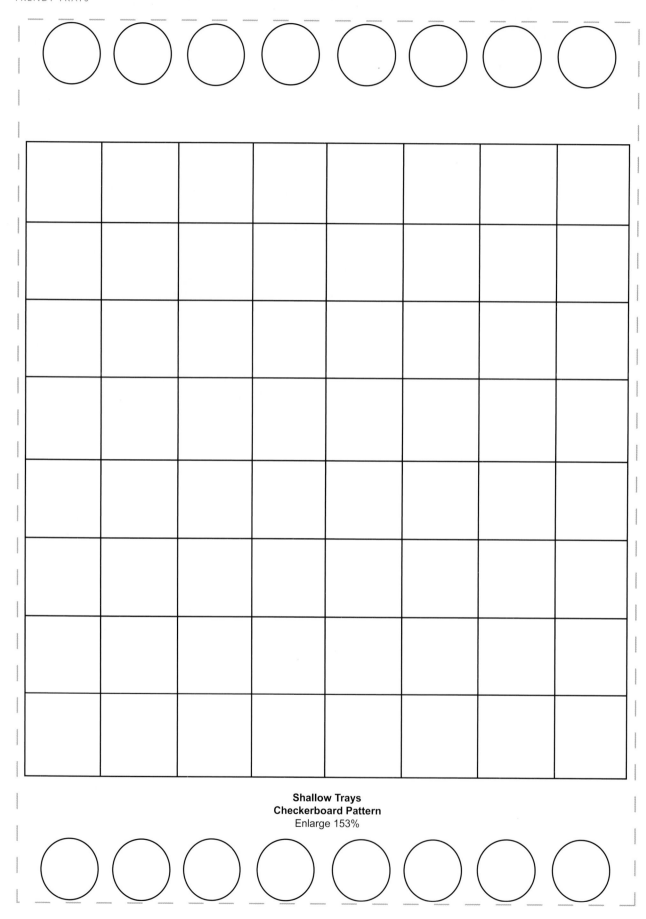

Shallow Trays
Checkerboard Pattern
Enlarge 153%

STACKABLE
BOXES

Designs by Wayne and Rhonda Sutter
Decorative finishes by Cathy Becker, OSCI

Toys, books, file folders, towels, collectibles … the possibilities for these stackable cubes are endless! The varied finishes add personality to simple plywood boxes.

PROJECT SIZE
12x12x12 inches

TOOLS
- Table saw or circular saw
- Drill
- Nail set

SUPPLIES FOR ONE BOX
- ¾-inch oak plywood: 2x4-foot sheet
- Iron-on wood edging tape
- Finish nails
- Wood putty
- Sandpaper

For Oak Stackable Boxes
- Swing Paints Circa 1850 Exterior Varnish
- Swing Paints Circa 1850 Fine Wood Stain
- Swing Paints Circa 1850 Fast Dry Polyurethane
- Swing Paints Klenk's Nu-Lustre-55
- Swing Paints Circa 1850 Stain 'n Varnish
- Mineral spirits
- Turpentine
- Lint-free cloth, pure bristle brush or lambskin applicator
- Fine steel wool

For Memory Keepsake Boxes
- Photocopies of photographs and memorabilia
- Plaid sepia #2052 Royalcoat

Decoupage Finish
- Plaid FolkArt Finishes matte #773 Aerosol Lacquer

For Kids' Cubbies
- Plaid Patricia Nimocks Clear Acrylic Sealer
- Plaid FolkArt acrylic paint: wicker white #901, school bus yellow #736, engine red #436, sterling blue #441, licorice #938, thicket #924, grass green #644, berry wine #434 and warm white #649
- Plaid FolkArt Glazing Medium
- Graphite paper
- ABC border stencil
- Plaid FolkArt Artist's Pigments: yellow ochre #AP917, pure orange #AP628 and dioxazine purple #AP463
- Plaid FolkArt One Stroke paintbrushes: ¾-inch flat, #12 flat, #2 script liner, regular scruffy and #2 flat
- Plaid wall weaver faux-finish brush #30112
- Plaid spouncer set #4154
- Plaid detail painters #4156
- Scotch brand Magic tape

For Teen Organizers
- Plaid Patricia Nimocks Clear Acrylic Sealer
- Plaid FolkArt acrylic paint: fuchsia #635, lime yellow #478, warm

white #649 and licorice #938
- Plaid FolkArt Artist's Pigments: aqua #AP481 and pure orange #AP628
- Plaid FolkArt Floating Medium
- Plaid FolkArt One Stroke paintbrushes: ¾-inach flat and #2 script liner
- Plaid Stencil Decor ¼-inch dauber set
- Scotch brand Magic tape
- Graphite paper

For Patio Boxes
- Plaid Patricia Nimocks Clear Acrylic Sealer
- Plaid FolkArt acrylic paint: wicker white #901, purple passion #638, raspberry sherbet #966, linen #420, olive green #449, basil green #645 and butter pecan #939
- Plaid FolkArt Artist's Pigments: warm white #AP649, yellow ochre #AP917 and burnt umber #AP462
- Plaid FolkArt One Stroke Ferns #4301 Adhesive Background Template
- Plaid Stencil Decor ¼-inch dauber set
- Plaid One Stroke paintbrushes: ¾-inch flat, #12 flat and #2 script liner
- Floating medium

Box No.1

Box No.2

Box No.3

OAK STACKABLE
BOXES

91 FAST DRY POLY

This clear, tough coating protects and beautifies all interior wood surfaces including floors, cabinets, doors, furniture and panelling. Circa 1850 Fast Dry Polyurethane by Swing Paints can be recoated in as little as three hours and cures to an exceptionally hard finish.

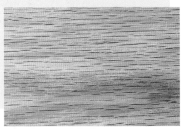

92 EXTERIOR VARNISH

This exterior varnish has a unique tung oil formula that provides a breathable, water-repellent finish on all exterior wood surfaces. Circa 1850 Exterior Varnish by Swing Paints screens out harmful UV rays and also incorporates a fungicide and mildewcide.

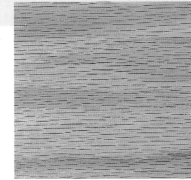

93 FINE WOOD STAIN

This product highlights the natural grain of the wood without causing grain rise. Circa 1850 Fine Wood Stain by Swing Paints provides uniform staining on all unfinished interior wood surfaces and cleans up easily with water.

CUTTING

1 From ¾-inch oak plywood, cut two 12x12-inch pieces (A) for top and bottom, two 10½x12-inch pieces (C) for sides, and one 10½x10½-inch piece (B) for back.

ASSEMBLE

1 Following manufacturer's directions, apply iron-on wood edge tape to all four edges of top and bottom (A) and to front and back (10½-inch) edges of sides (C).

2 Nail top (A) to 12-inch edge of one side (C). *Note: Top should overlap side, with edges flush.* Nail back (B) to top and side with back edges flush. Nail remaining side (C) and then bottom (A) in place.

3 Set nails. Fill holes with wood putty; let dry. Sand surfaces smooth and remove dustt.

Finishes
OAK STACKABLE BOXES
Box No. 1

1 Sand to obtain a smooth, uniform surface; remove dust.

2 Thin Fast Dry Polyurethane with 10 percent mineral spirits for first coat. Wipe or brush on a thin coat using a lint-free cloth, pure bristle brush or a lamb-skin applicator. Apply evenly with long strokes in the direction of the grain.

3 Allow to dry for at least three hours, then sand lightly using very fine sandpaper or steel wool.

4 Remove all dust and apply a second coat as above. If a third coat is desired, resand and apply as above.

Box No.5

Box No.4

OAK STACKABLE BOXES

94 STAIN AND VARNISH COMBO

This unique gel formula maintains a consistent blend of stain and varnish with no mixing or stirring required, ensuring uniformity from beginning to end. Circa 1850 Stain 'n Varnish by Swing Paints goes on without runs, drips or brush marks and can be used on virtually any surface.

95 EPOXY FINISH

This thick, high-gloss finish equals up to 55 coats of varnish and can be applied over a variety of surfaces. Klenk's Nu-Lustre 55 by Swing Paints is a two-part finish that needs to cure for at least 24 hours after application.

Box No. 2

1 Sand to obtain a smooth, uniform surface; remove dust.

2 For the first coat, thin the Exterior Varnish with 10-25 percent turpentine.

3 Apply a thin coat of varnish, with long, even strokes in the direction of the grain, using a pure bristle brush. Allow to dry for 24 hours, then apply a second coat. Allow to dry, then apply a third coat if desired.

Box No. 3

1 Sand to obtain a smooth, uniform surface; remove dust.

2 Apply Fine Wood Stain with a brush or cloth. Wait 10 minutes then wipe off excess. Apply a second coat after 12 hours.

3 Thin Fast Dry Polyurethane with 10 percent mineral spirits for first coat. Wipe or brush on a thin coat using a lint-free cloth, pure bristle brush or a lambskin applicator. Apply evenly with long strokes in the direction of the grain.

4 Allow to dry for at least three hours, then sand lightly using very fine sandpaper or steel wool.

5 Remove all dust and apply a second coat as above. If a third coat is desired, re-sand and apply as above.

Box No. 4

1 Sand to obtain a smooth, uniform surface; remove dust.

2 With a lint-free cloth, spread a generous coat of Stain 'n Varnish over the surface and wipe off excess immediately. Rub evenly in the direction of the grain. Let dry eight hours.

3 Smooth lightly with fine steel wool.

4 Using a cloth slightly dampened with Stain'n Varnish, rub lightly with quick, full-length strokes in the direction of the grain. Continue until there is no drag on the cloth and the surface is smooth.

Box No. 5

1 Sand to obtain a smooth, uniform surface; remove dust.

2 Using Klenk's Nu-Lustre-55, measure one part resin to one part hardener in separate containers. Stir vigorously for about two minutes. Empty the contents of one container into the second container. Mix thoroughly for 60 seconds and pour onto the wood surface immediately. Bubbles that rise to the surface may be broken by gently exhaling on them. Let dry for 24 hours.

MEMORY KEEPSAKE BOXES

1 Cut out photocopied photos and memorabilia.

2 Apply a light coat of decoupage finish to back of design; smooth onto box. Repeat to cover outside of box. Let dry.

3 Following manufacturer's directions, apply three coats of decoupage medium over entire surface, letting dry after each application.

4 Seal with several coats of spray lacquer following manufacturer's directions.

KIDS' CUBBIES

1 Spray surfaces with sealer; let dry. Sand lightly and remove dust.

2 Using a damp 2-inch flat paintbrush, apply three coats of warm white to box, letting dry after each coat.

3 Draw a light pencil line 1½ inches from edges on each side of box. Place tape along inside edge of pencil line.

4 Mix sterling blue with a tablespoon of glaze; paint 1½-inch border on one side of box. Use wall weaver brush to comb through paint vertically, then horizontally, and then again vertically, wiping off bristles after each stroke to create crayon look. Let dry. Remove tape.

5 Repeat step 4 on remaining three sides of box, using school bus yellow, engine red and grass green.

MEMORY KEEPSAKE BOXES

56 FAUX FABRIC DECOUPAGE
Use Plaid's Royal Coat decoupage finish with elegant rolled wrapping paper, photocopies or wallpaper to create this trendy look. Royal Coat decoupage is acid free and dries quickly to a hard, satin finish.

6 Referring to Figs. 1–4 for placement, use ¾-inch spouncer to stencil alphabet letters as follows: A, engine red; B, grass green; C, school bus yellow; D, sterling blue; E, engine red; F, grass green; G, school bus yellow; H, sterling blue; I, engine red; J, school bus yellow; K, engine red; and L, sterling blue.

7 Transfer pattern designs to sides of boxes using graphite paper; paint as follows using acrylic paints and pigments:

Ant—Use a damp ¾-inch flat paintbrush and *licorice* to paint body; let dry. With *wicker white*, paint eyes and mouth and add highlights on top of body; let dry. Paint pupils on eyes with *licorice*, and highlight with *wicker white*.

Bumblebee—Load the bottom of a dry scruffy brush with *school bus yellow*; paint body of bee by pouncing brush up and down; let dry. Load scruffy brush with *licorice* and pounce stripes on body; pounce head in a circular motion. Completely load the ¾-inch flat brush with *wicker white*, then side-load a little *licorice* with the white to create a soft gray; paint the two large wings with a teardrop stroke, and the back smaller wings using a chisel stroke. Let dry. Paint eyes and mouth *wicker white*. Thin *licorice* with water to the consistency of ink; using script liner, outline wings, add vein lines, antennae and feet, and add *licorice* to eyes. Dip the tip of paintbrush handle in *licorice* and dot tops of antennae.

KIDS' CUBBIES

96 CRAYON LOOK
A special combing tool gives the look and feel of a child's crayon. It's fun and easy to achieve.

97 ONE-STROKE PAINTING
This technique, made famous by decorative painter Donna Dewberry, makes it easy for anyone to paint like a pro!

TEEN ORGANIZERS

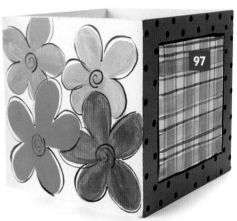

Caterpillar—Pounce one side of the 1¾-inch spouncer into *grass green*, and the other side into *thicket*; with the darker color at the bottom, pounce the five circles of the caterpillar's body, twisting the handle of the spouncer to create a full circle. Let dry. Load the script liner with *licorice* and paint the eyes, mouth and antennae; let dry. Dot the tops of the antennae as for bumblebee. Thin *wicker white* to the consistency of ink and use script liner to add dots in the eyes and a comma stroke on top of each circle.

Daisy—Double-load the ¾-inch flat brush with *yellow ochre* and *school bus yellow*; paint chisel strokes toward the center of the daisy, forming a complete circle. Wipe brush on a paper towel and reload with *school bus yellow* and *wicker white*; paint the same chisel stroke over the top of the first layer. Dip the bottom of one side of the ¾-inch spouncer into *grass green*, and the other side into *thicket*; pounce into center of daisy. Double-load #2 flat brush with *grass green* and *thicket*;

paint stem, wiggle leaves and one-stroke leaf.

Eggs—Double-load ¾-inch flat brush with *fuchsia* and *wicker white*; paint shape of left egg, keeping fuchsia side of the brush to the outside. Double-load brush again with *pure orange* and *wicker white*; paint shape of top egg, keeping pure orange to the outside. Double-load brush again with *dioxazine purple* and *wicker white*; paint shape of right egg, keeping purple to the outside. Thin *grass green* to the consistency of ink; paint lines on fuchsia egg. Thin *berry wine* and *dioxazine purple*; paint stripes on pure orange egg using script liner. Thin *wicker white* and *sterling blue*; paint X's on purple egg with wicker white, and stripes with sterling blue. Double-load #12 flat brush with *fuchsia* and *wicker white*; paint hay using chisel edge.

Fish—*Note: Use ¾-inch flat brush double-loaded with pure orange and school bus yellow throughout, unless otherwise stated.* Paint main oval shape

98 PAINTED PLAID
Using a flat brush and bright colors, you can create an easy plaid design without a pattern.

the bottom, pounce and twist dauber to create each grape. Load script liner with burnt umber to paint stems, working outward from grapes; paint tendrils with same brush. Double-load #12 flat brush with thicket and grass green; paint wiggle one-stroke leaves. Load script liner with wicker white and paint highlights on right sides of some grapes.

Heart—Double-load ¾-inch flat brush with berry wine and wicker white; paint heart, keeping berry wine to the outside. Let dry. Use script liner and thinned wicker white to paint lettering and highlight.

Ice cream—Double-load ¾-inch flat brush with butter pecan and school bus yellow; side-load wicker white on the yellow side to soften. Paint triangle shape for cone; let dry. Load #12 flat brush with burnt umber and wicker white to paint crisscross lines using chisel edge of brush. Load half of 1¾-inch spouncer into burnt umber and the other have in wicker white; pounce and twist onto ice cream to cover. Load ¾-inch pouncer with berry wide and wicker white; pounce and twist onto cherry. Load script liner with burnt umber; paint stem on cherry. Use script liner and wicker white to paint highlights on cherry, ice cream and cone.

Jelly fish—Completely load ¾-inch flat brush with floating medium; side-load one side into berry wine and blend. Paint jellyfish, keeping berry wine to outside. Let dry. Use chisel edge of same brush to paint tentacles. Load script liner with thinned wicker white to paint eyes. Use script liner and licorice to outline eyes, paint eyebrows and

of fish first, keeping orange to the outside. Beginning at top left side of fish, paint top fins with chisel strokes coming from body out; continue until you have a solid area at the top right-hand side. Paint tail with two seashell strokes connected together at the sides. For bottom fin, paint small, one-stroke leaves coming from body. Paint fin on body with a seashell stroke. Dip ¼-inch dauber in *sterling blue* and dab on for eye; let dry. Load script liner with

thinned *sterling blue* to paint detail on fish. Load #12 flat brush with *engine red*; paint lips using chisel strokes toward fish. Dip tip of script liner in *licorice* and dot center of fish eye; highlight with a dot of *wicker white* when dry.

Grapes—Dip half of the bottom of the ¼-inch dauber into dioxazine purple, and the other half into wicker white. Working from the top of the grapes to

PATIO BOXES

81 STENCIL
A purchased stencil allows you to quickly add a detailed background to any large area.

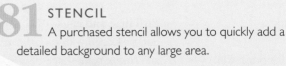

inside of mouth. Paint teeth white and tongue engine red.

Kite—Completely loading #12 flat brush with each color, paint bottom left portion school bus yellow, top left portion pure orange, bottom right portion sterling blue and top right portion engine red. Load script liner with thinned licorice to paint braces of kite and string. Using #6 flat brush and alternating colors, paint bows with one-stroke leaf strokes in direction of string.

Ladybug—Double-load ¾-inch flat brush with engine red and berry wine; paint body, keeping berry wine to the outside. Load script liner with thinned licorice to paint head, line down middle of back, legs, antennae and portion under wings. Load script liner with thinned wicker white to paint highlights on body and head.

TEEN ORGANIZERS

1 Spray surfaces with sealer; let dry. Sand lightly and remove dust.

2 Using a damp 2-inch flat paintbrush, apply three coats of warm white to box, letting dry after each coat.

Aqua plaid

1 Draw a light pencil line 1½ inches from edges of box. Place tape along inside edge of pencil line. Referring to photo for placement, use ¾-inch flat brush to paint plaid design as follows:

Wide yellow stripes—Load brush with *lime yellow* and floating medium; paint wide stripes across box within taped edges.

Narrow orange stripes—Load brush with *pure orange*; use chisel edge to paint a narrow line on each side of each wide yellow stripe.

Wide pink stripes—Turn box 90 degrees. Load brush with *fuchsia* and floating medium; paint wide stripes across box, perpendicular to yellow and orange stripes.

Narrow blue stripes—Load brush with *aqua*; use chisel edge to paint a narrow line on each side of each wide fuchsia stripe.

2 Carefully remove tape; let paint dry. Completely load ¾-inch flat brush with aqua and paint outside border; let dry. Remove tape.

3 Load ¾-inch flat brush with licorice; outline plaid area using chisel edge.

4 Completely load ¼-inch dauber with licorice; place dots randomly around outside border.

Fuchsia plaid

1 Draw a light pencil line 1½ inches from edges of box. Place tape along outside edge of pencil line. Repeat step 1 of aqua plaid.

2 Carefully remove tape; let paint dry. Completely load ¾-inch flat brush with fuchsia and paint outside border;

let dry. Remove tape.

3 Load ¾-inch flat brush with licorice; paint border between plaid and aqua area using chisel edge.

Flowers

1 Transfer flower pattern to box, overlapping petals as shown.

2 Completely loading 1½-inch brush with each color, paint flowers using lime yellow, fuchsia, aqua and pure orange alternately. Let dry.

3 Load script liner with thinned licorice; outline flowers and paint spiral centers.

PATIO BOXES

1 Spray surfaces with sealer; let dry. Sand lightly and remove dust.

2 Using a damp 2-inch flat paintbrush, apply three coats of warm white to box, letting dry after each coat.

3 Position ferns background template on box as desired and paint with a pouncing motion using ⅝-inch spouncer and linen. Repeat to cover sides of box. Let dry.

4 Use graphite paper to transfer vine patterns to sides of boxes. ***Note:*** *Pattern No. 3 is on side of bottom box, pattern No. 2 is on side of top box and pattern No. 1 is on top of top box. Paint design as follows:*

Vine—Double-load ¾-inch flat brush with *burnt umber* and *linen*; using chisel edge of brush, paint vine across sides and top of boxes.

Bird nest and eggs—With same brush double-loaded with *burnt umber* and *linen*, paint shape of next with a very wide, short rosebud shape. Let dry. Completely load #12 flat brush with *burnt umber*, and side-load with *wicker white*; paint eggs. Completely load #12 flat brush with floating medium, and side-load with *burnt umber*; shade behind eggs. Load script liner alternately with *linen, yellow ochre, wicker white* and *burnt umber* to paint wispy grasses of nest.

Wiggle leaves—Double-load ¾-inch flat brush with olive green and basil; paint large leaves.

Rosebuds—Double-load #12 flat brush with raspberry sherbet and *wicker white*; paint rosebuds.

Cascading purple flowers—Double-load #12 flat brush with *purple passion* and *wicker white*; paint flowers with teardrop strokes.

One-stroke leaves and calyx—Double-load #12 flat brush with *olive green* and *basil*; paint simple one-stroke leaves and calyx of flowers.

 to consistency of ink and paint tendrils with script liner. ✻

**Stackable Boxes
Kids' Cubbies
Fig. 1**

**Stackable Boxes
Kids' Cubbies
Ant**

**Stackable Boxes
Kids' Cubbies
Catterpillar**

**Stackable Boxes
Kids' Cubbies
Bee**

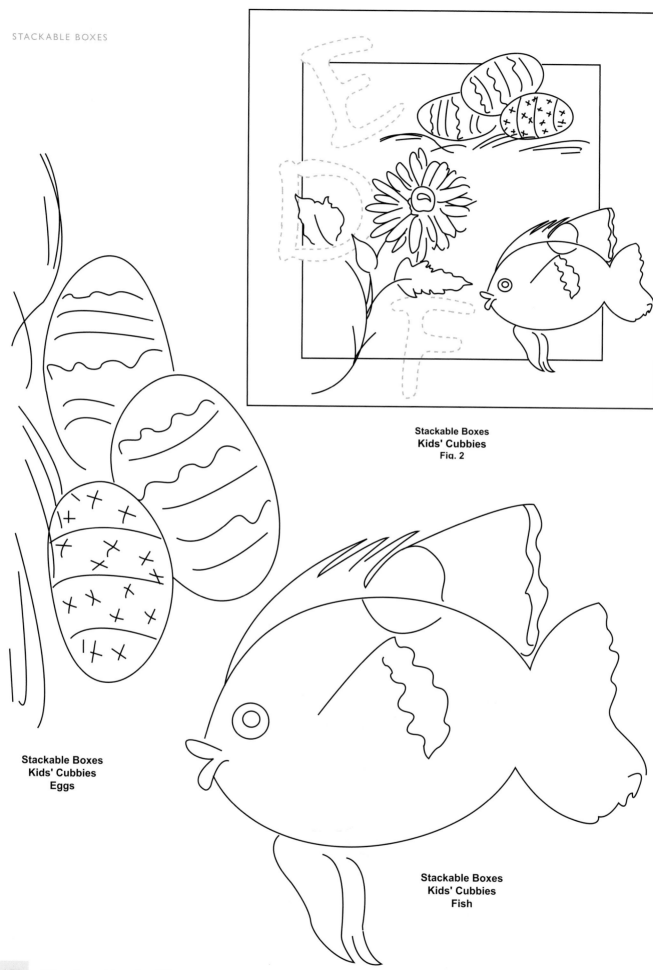

Stackable Boxes
Kids' Cubbies
Fig. 2

Stackable Boxes
Kids' Cubbies
Eggs

Stackable Boxes
Kids' Cubbies
Fish

**Stackable Boxes
Kids' Cubbies
Daisy**

**Stackable Boxes
Kids' Cubbies
Grapes**

**Stackable Boxes
Kids' Cubbies
Fig. 3**

**Stackable Boxes
Kids' Cubbies
Ice Cream**

**Stackable Boxes
Kids' Cubbies
Heart**

**Stackable Boxes
Kids' Cubbies
Fig. 4**

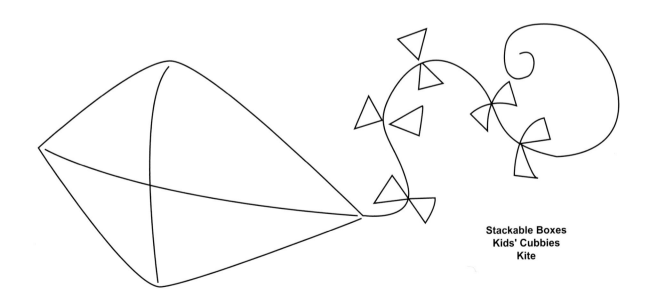

**Stackable Boxes
Kids' Cubbies
Kite**

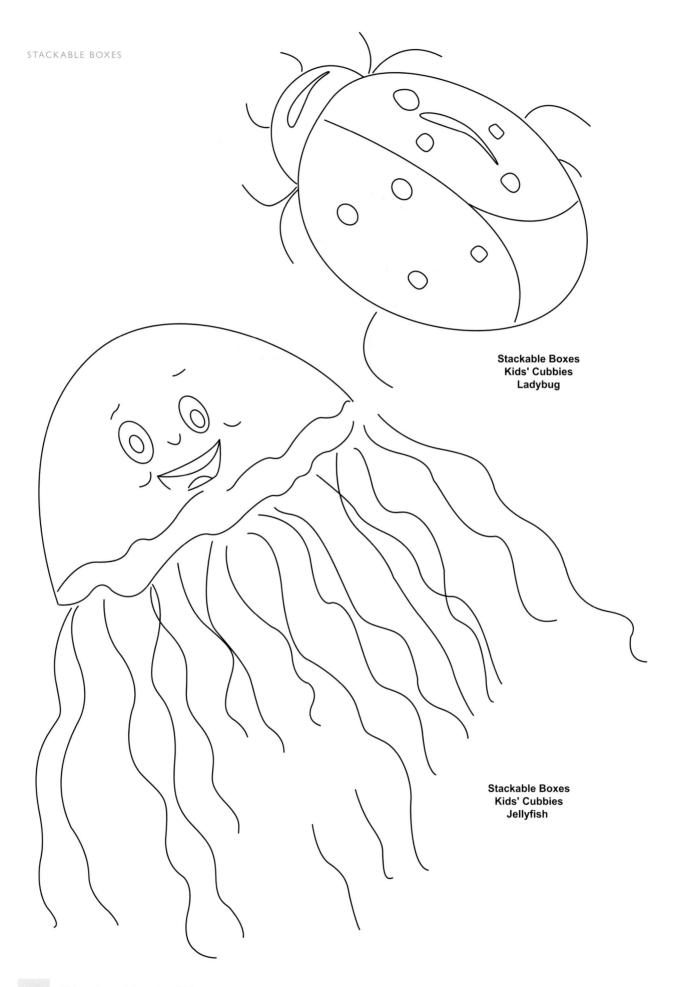

**Stackable Boxes
Kids' Cubbies
Ladybug**

**Stackable Boxes
Kids' Cubbies
Jellyfish**

Stackable Boxes
Vertical Patio Boxes
Right Vine No. 1
Join to left Vine No. 1
at dashed lines

Stackable Boxes
Vertical Patio Boxes
Left Vine No. 1
Join to right Vine No. 1
at dashed lines

Stackable Boxes
Patio Boxes
Vine No. 3 Leaf
Join to Vine No. 3 top
at dashed lines

Stackable Boxes
Patio Boxes
Top Vine No. 3
Join to Vine No. 3 leaf and
bottom Vine No. 3 at dashed lines

Stackable Boxes
Patio Boxes
Bottom Vine No. 3
Join to top Vine No. 3
at dashed lines

**Stackable Boxes
Vertical Patio Boxes
Right Vine No. 2**
Join to left Vine No. 2
at dashed lines

Stackable Boxes
Vertical Patio Boxes
Left Vine No. 2
Join to right Vine No. 2
at dashed lines

GIVE US
THIS DAY

Designs by Wayne Sutter
Decorative Painting by Cathy Becker OSCI

Store baked goods out of sight but within easy reach of the breakfast table with these handy bread boxes. Choose a natural finish or try your hand at decorative painting.

CUTTING

1 From 1x6 pine, cut one 16-inch length (A) for top, and two 7½-inch lengths (B) for sides.

2 From 1x8 pine, cut one 17-inch length (D) for bottom.

3 Rip-cut remaining 1x8 to 6¾-inch width; cut two 14⁷⁄₁₆-inch lengths (C) for back and door.

4 Using table saw or hand plane, bevel front edge of top and bottom edge of door to 14 degrees. Using miter gauge, cut one edge of each side at a 14-degree angle.

5 Using router with ¼-inch round over bit, round both sides of top edge of door, and top sides only of bottom on sides and front. **Note:** *Do not round back edge of bottom.*

ASSEMBLE

1 Referring to assembly diagram and Fig. 1, glue and nail top (A) to sides (B); glue and nail back (C) to top and sides with edges flush. Wipe off excess glue. Set nails and fill holes with matching wood filler; let dry.

2 Glue and nail assembled top/sides/back to bottom (D) with back edges flush. Wipe off excess glue.

3 Tape door (C) in place. Using drill with brad point bit, drill 2-inch-deep holes through sides into door for inserting dowels for hinges. **Note:** *Carefully align holes as they are drilled. The holes must be drilled straight for the door to swing on dowels smoothly.*

PROJECT SIZE

17x7x7¼ inches

TOOLS

- Table saw or circular saw
- Hand plane (optional)
- Miter gauge
- Router with ¼-inch roundover bit
- Nail set
- Drill with brad point bit
- Orbital sander (hand sander, optional)

SUPPLIES FOR ONE BOX

- 1x6 pine: 3 feet
- 1x8 pine: 4 feet
- ¼-inch wooden dowel: two 1½-inch lengths
- 1-inch brads
- Wood glue
- Wood filler to match finish
- Masking tape
- 1-inch wooden knob with wood screw

For Grandma's Bread Box

- Black Bison Fine Paste Wax by Liberon
- Sealer

For Simply Pine Bread Box

- Bullseye Shellac by Zinsser
- Sealer

For Good Morning Bread Box

- Plaid FolkArt Sanding Sealer
- Fine-grade sandpaper or steel wool
- Plaid FolkArt acrylic paint: sunflower #432, berry wine #434, engine red #436, heartland blue #608, school bus yellow #736, wicker white #901, tapioca #903, thicket #924, licorice #938 and honeycomb #942
- Plaid FolkArt Extender
- Plaid Folk-Art One-Stroke paintbrushes: ¾-inch flat, #12 script, #2 script liner, #8 flat, #6 flat and #2 flat
- Graphite paper
- Plaid FolkArt artists pigments: Hauser green light #AP459, burnt umber #AP462, pure orange #AP628, burnt Carmine #AP686 and yellow ochre #AP917
- Plaid FolkArt floating medium
- Plaid FolkArt brown antiquing polish
- Plaid FolkArt matte lacquer
- Old toothbrush
- Mini scruffy brush

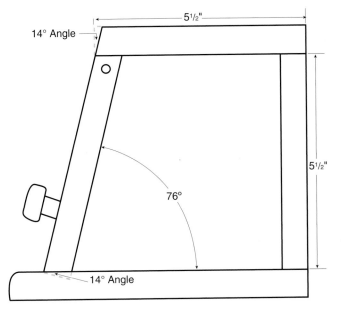

14° Angle

5½"

76°

14° Angle

5½"

Bread Boxes
Fig. 1

	GIVE US THIS DAY CUTTING CHART (Actual Sizes)			
P	T	W	L	#
A	¾"	5½"	16"	1
B	¾"	5½"	7½"	2
C	¾"	6¾"	14⁷⁄₁₆"	2
D	¾"	7¼"	17"	1

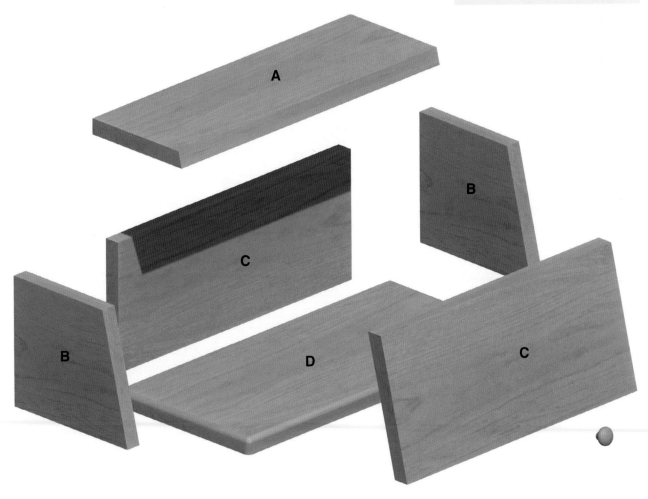

A

C

B

B

D

C

end grain areas until the wood stops absorbing the shellac. Wipe off any excess with a cloth dampened with alcohol.

3 Let dry 20 minutes. Sand lightly and remove dust before additional coats are applied.

GOOD MORNING BREAD BOX

1 Spray surfaces with sealer; let dry. Sand lightly and remove dust.

2 *Note: For smoother coverage, use a damp brush for base-coating. Apply two or three coats to cover, letting dry after each coat.* Base-coat inside of bread box with a mixture of one part burnt umber and two parts extender; let dry. Apply three coats of tapioca to outside top and sides of box, letting dry after each coat. Base-coat bottom edges and box bottom with licorice.

3 Squeeze a small portion of burnt umber onto old toothbrush dampened with water. Tap the head of the brush on a tabletop to force the paint down into the bristles, then spatter the paint onto the bread box by pulling bristles back with thumb nail. Repeat process with licorice. Let dry.

4 Use graphite paper to transfer large oval shape onto center front of door; transfer smaller oval shapes onto box sides. Base-coat ovals with licorice. Let dry. Transfer rooster design to front of box. Transfer vegetables to sides of box; base-coat vegetables with wicker white. Referring to artist's worksheets, paint designs as follows:

Straw—Double-load ¾-inch flat brush

4 Remove tape and dry-fit dowels. Trim door, if necessary. Apply glue to end of each dowel that will remain in side of box; insert dowels. Let dry.

5 Sand surfaces smooth and remove dust. Drill hole on center front of door approximately 1½ inches from bottom edge; attach wooden knob with screw.

Finishes

GRANDMA'S BREAD BOX

1 Spray surfaces with sealer; let dry. Sand lightly and remove dust.

2 Using a clean rag, scoop some wax out of the container and wrap it within a thin layer of the rag. Apply the wax using light, circular strokes through a layer of rag.

3 Let dry for 15 minutes, then buff the shelf using a clean portion of the rag.

SIMPLY PINE BREAD BOX

1 Spray surfaces with sealer; let dry. Sand lightly and remove dust.

2 Flood the shellac liberally onto the wood, letting it soak into any

GRANDMA'S BREAD BOX

99 FINE FURNITURE WAX

A balanced blend of natural and mineral waxes, Black Bison Fine Paste Wax by Liberon polishes wood and helps prevent it from drying out. It is useful on all types of wood, particularly fine and antique furniture.

with *yellow ochre* and *sunflower*; use chisel edge to paint straw, occasionally adding *burnt umber* to yellow ochre side and *wicker white* to sunflower side for contrast.

Rooster chest and belly—Double-load #8 flat brush with *honeycomb* and *sunflower* to paint chest and belly with soft, curving upward strokes, leading with sunflower (Nos. 1 and 2). Occasionally side load *burnt umber* on honeycomb side and *wicker white* on sunflower side as you work, for contrast.

Rooster blue tail feathers—Double-load *heartland blue* and *wicker white* on #8 flat brush. Use chisel edge, leading with wicker white, to paint high, back tail feathers with a sweeping motion (No. 3).

Rooster green tail feathers and wing—Double-load *Hauser green light*

and *thicket* on #8 flat brush (Nos. 4 and 5).

Rooster neck feathers—Double-load *wicker white* and *honeycomb* on #8 flat brush; use chisel edge, leading with wicker white, to paint neck feathers, overlapping body and wing (No. 6).

Rooster comb and wattle—Double-load #6 flat brush with *berry wine* and *engine red*. Paint comb and wattle with berry wine towards outside; let dry. Repeat step, if needed, for coverage.

Rooster beak—Load #2 flat brush with *wicker white*; base-coat beak. Let dry. Double-load #2 flat brush with *yellow ochre* and *burnt umber*; paint beak again.

Rooster eye—Dot eye with *licorice* loaded on #2 script liner; let dry. Add small *yellow ochre* dot, then a very small dot of *wicker white* for highlight.

Rooster carrots—Double-load #8 flat brush with *pure orange* and *burnt carmine*. Repeat if needed for complete coverage. Completely load #2 flat brush with floating medium and side-load with *burnt umber* to shade carrots. Completely load #2 script liner with *Hauser green light*; paint stems from top of carrots. Double-load mini scruffy brush with *Hauser green light* and *thicket*; pounce carrot leaves.

Rooster leeks—Load #6 flat brush with *wicker white*, then side-load with *Hauser green light*; paint bottom portion of leek. Double-load #6 flat brush with *Hauser green light* and *thicket*; paint green stems. Load #6 flat with floating medium, then side-load with *burnt umber*; shade between and under leeks. Completely load #2 script liner with thinned *wicker white*; paint root hairs from bottoms of leeks.

Rooster corn—Completely load #8

flat brush with *school bus yellow*, then side-load with *wicker white*; paint oval shape of cob. Load one side of #12 brush with *wicker white*; paint kernels with over-the-hill strokes. Double-load ¾-inch flat brush with *Hauser green light* and *thicket*, then side-load with *burnt carmine*; paint corn husks.

Peas—Double-load #12 flat brush with *Hauser green light* and *thicket*; paint base of pea pod. Side-load a little *burnt carmine* on one side of #12 flat brush and paint opposing C strokes to form peas. Reload #12 flat brush with *Hauser green light* and *thicket* and pull cover strokes across the peas.

Pea blossom and leaves—Completely load #12 flat brush with floating medium, then side-load with *wicker white*; paint blossom using five-petal flower stroke. Dot center with tip of script liner dipped in *school bus yellow*. Double-load #12 flat brush with *thicket and Hauser green light*; paint one stroke leaves.

Corn—Completely load ¾-inch flat brush with *school bus yellow*, then side-load with *wicker white*; paint oval shape of cob. Load *wicker white* on one side of #12 brush; paint kernels with over-the-hill strokes. Double-load ¾-inch flat brush with *Hauser green light* and *thicket*, then side-load with

burnt carmine; paint corn husks.

5 Completely load ¾-inch flat brush with floating medium, then side-load with burnt umber; shade around each oval, with burnt umber edge of brush to the outside.

6 Allow paint to dry completely. Place a little brown antiquing polish on a soft dry cloth; wipe polish on edges of bread box and lightly across painted surfaces.

7 Spray outside of box with matte lacquer, following manufacturer's directions. ✺

SIMPLY PINE BREAD BOX

100

100 SHELLAC

All-natural, non-toxic and easy to use, Bullseye Shellac by Zinsser dries dust-free in minutes and is UV resistant.

**GOOD MORNING
BREAD BOX**

101

101 SPLATTER

Dip an old toothbrush or stencil brush into paint, then rub your thumb over wet paint to flick small droplets of paint over the surface. The size and shape of the splatters can be varied by the speed with which you rub your thumb and how close the brush is to the work.

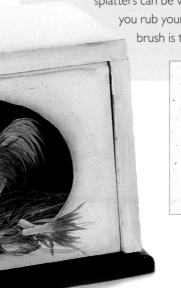

Painting techniques for Good Morning Bread Box

ROOSTER

HAY

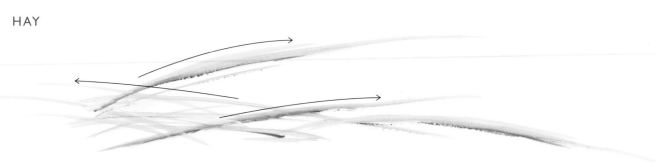

CARROT

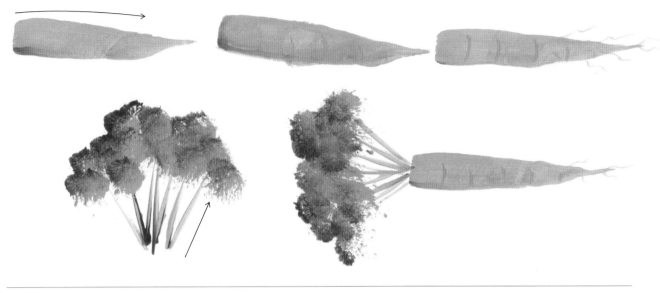

CELERY

CORN

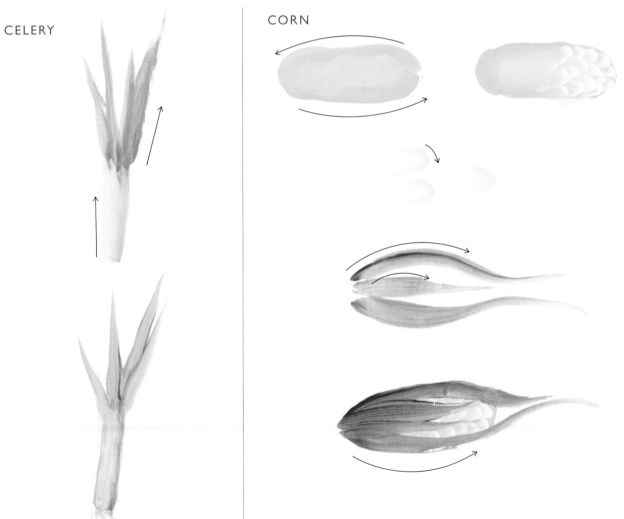

LEAVES

PEAS

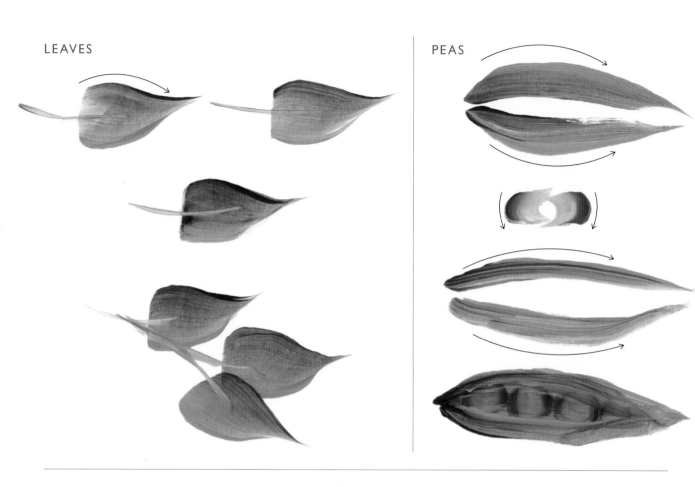

FLOWER

Bread Boxes
Good Morning Bread Box
Peas

Bread Boxes
Good Morning Bread Box
Corn

Bread Boxes
Good Morning Bread Box
Rooster

FINISHES INDEX

Standard Lumber Dimensions

NOMINAL	ACTUAL	METRIC
1" x 2"	¾" x 1½"	19 x 38 mm
1" x 3"	¾" x 2½"	19 x 64 mm
1" x 4"	¾" x 3½"	19 x 89 mm
1" x 5"	¾" x 4½"	19 x 114 mm
1" x 6"	¾" x 5½"	19 x 140 mm
1" x 7"	¾" x 6¼"	19 x 159 mm
1" x 8"	¾" x 7¼"	19 x 184 mm
1" x 10"	¾" x 9¼"	19 x 235 mm
1" x 12"	¾" x 11¼"	19 x 286 mm
1¼" x 4"	1" x 3½"	25 x 89 mm
1¼" x 6"	1" x 5½"	25 x 140 mm
1¼" x 8"	1" x 7¼"	25 x 184 mm
1¼" x 10"	1" x 9¼"	25 x 235 mm
1¼" x 12"	1" x 11¼"	25 x 286 mm
1½" x 4"	1¼" x 3½"	32 x 89 mm
1½" x 6"	1¼" x 5½"	32 x 140 mm
1½" x 8"	1¼" x 7¼"	32 x 184 mm
1½" x 10"	1¼" x 9¼"	32 x 235 mm
1½" x 12"	1¼" x 11¼"	32 x 286 mm
2" x 3"	1½" x 2½"	38 x 64 mm
2" x 4"	1½" x 3½"	38 x 89 mm
2" x 6"	1½" x 5½"	38 x 140 mm
2" x 8"	1½" x 7¼"	38 x 184 mm
2" x 10"	1½" x 9¼"	38 x 235 mm
2" x 12"	1½" x 11¼"	38 x 286 mm
3" x 6"	2½" x 5½"	64 x 140 mm
4" x 4"	3½" x 3½"	89 x 89 mm
4" x 6"	3½" x 5½"	89 x 140 mm

SPECIAL THANKS

We thank the talented woodworking designers whose work is featured in this collection.

Joyce Atwood
Americana Bench, 28
Embossed Stucco Bench, 28
Whitewashed Bench, 28

Cathy Becker OSCI
Good Morning Breadbox, 162
Kids' Cubbies, 141
Memory Keepsake Boxes, 141
Patio Boxes, 141
Teen Organizers, 141

June Fiechter
Copper & Steel
   Plant Stand, 81
Floral Fabric Bench, 74
Faux Stone Table, 101
Faux Mosaic Table, 101
Marble Plant Stand, 81
Western Star Bench, 74

Barbara Greve,
Denim Look Shelf, 13
Roller Spots Shelf, 13
Snakeskin Shelf, 13

Loretta Mateik
Decoupaged Tea Tray, 90
Fanciful Fun, 66
Friends Frame, 46
Garden Sign, 20
Kid's Door Sign, 20
Marbled Frame, 46
Slip-Slap Frame, 46
Still Life Tea Tray, 90
Trailing Ivy Table, 66
Welcome Sign, 20

LuAnn Nelson
Beach House Frame, 35
Cherry Veneer Frame, 35
Fleur de Lis Frame, 35
Maple Burl & Birch
   Veneer Frame, 35
Mystique Frame, 35
Sparkling Sand Frame, 35
Stained Glass Frame, 35
Wood-Grained Frame, 35

Myra Risley Perrin
Good Luck Sconce, 85

Modern Metallic Sconce, 85
Walnut & Maple Sconce, 85

Patti J. Ryan
Antique Red Coat Rack, 107
Beach House Welcome
   Hall Tree, 107
Blue Skies Entry Mirror, 111
Game Board Tray, 136
Gilded Entry Mirror, 111
Leather Look Tray, 136
Mahogany Caddy, 96
Suede Caddy, 96

Wayne & Rhonda Sutter
Cherry Round &
   Pie Tables, 121
Good Morning Bread
   Box, 162
Grandma's Bread Box, 162
Kids' Cubbies, 141
Memory Keepsake Boxes, 141
Night & Day Round &
   Pie Tables, 121
Oak Round & Pie Tables, 121

Oak Stackable Boxes, 141
Patio Boxes, 141
Simply Pine Bread Box, 162
Teen Organizers, 141

Anna Thompson
Antique Walnut Cabinet, 58
Art Deco Plant Stand, 6
Beadboard Display Shelf, 131
Cherry Display Shelf, 131
Classic Cabinet, 116
Classic Cherry Drawers, 51
Colorful Kids' Drawers, 51
Easy Birch Drawers, 51
Natural Oak Plant Stand, 6
Old-Time Cabinet, 116
Rich Red Cabinet, 58
Sleek Black Cabinet, 58
Sunroom Plant Stand, 6

CONTACT INFORMATION

The following companies provided supplies for projects in *101 Ways to Finish Wood*. If you are unable to locate a product locally, contact the manufacturers listed below for the closest retail or mail-order source in your area.

Deco Art
www.decoart.com

Deft
(800) 544-3338
www.deftfinishes.com

Delta Technical Coatings
(800) 423-4135
www.deltacrafts.com

Design Master
www.dmcolor.com

Krylon
www.krylon.com

Golden Artist Colors
(607) 847-6154
www.goldenpaints.com

Liberon
www.liberon.co.nz

Marvy/Uchida
(800) 541-5877
www.marvy.com

Minwax
(800) 523-9299
www.minwax.com

Plaid Enterprises
(800) 842-4197
www.modpodge.com

Provo Craft
(800) 937-7686
www.provocraft.com

Rub n Buff
www.amaco.com

Sharpie
(800) 323-0749
www.sharpie.com

Swing Paints
www.swingpaints.com

Triangle Coatings
(800) 895-8000
www.tricoat.com

Wood-Kote
(800) 843-7666
www.woodkote.com

Zinsser
(732) 469-8100
www.zinsser.com